Mix a dose every hour, and whatever you do,
do not mix it with *ketamine* or *alcohol*.

THEY TEACH US HOW TO LIVE,
BUT WE ONLY LEARN HOW TO DIE.

An imprint of Voyaeon Publishing
1555 Vine St, Los Angeles, California 90028

Also available in a VOYAEON hardcover edition
Interior design by Mario Luxxor
Manufactured in the United States of America

To those friends who've died from an overdose. Their names I can't mention— or I'd be sued for defamation. But their absence forever *haunts* these pages.

LINCOLN

*"You think you're running from your home, but
you're really running from yourself."* Unknown

Lincoln sat on his bed, staring out of the
window—a habit reserved for moments of
deep contemplation or sadness. A sudden ring
shattered the silence, jerking him back to reality:
it was his father. 'Your mother has probably
spoken to you,' he said. 'I'm calling to ask—how
should I deal with Kathy? Swiftly or slowly?' He
meant poisoning—a gradual demise over the
course of the next few days.

Awakening abruptly, his body was drenched
in sweat, with tears flowing freely. In that instant,
he grappled with a pain so intense, crying like
a child. Strangely, he had neither a dog named
Kathy nor a mother nor a father in reality. Yet,
within the confines of his dream, those three

characters felt as tangible as his tears. Still dark, in that dusky moment, he gleaned a profound truth—we meet death either at the hand of God or at the whim of another.

———

Lincoln Sorni was born in a small and sweltering village in Mexico under circumstances of which he was unaware. When Lincoln was conceived, his parents were going through a tough time. His mother found out that her husband had another woman less than a mile away from their marital bed. She, the other woman, was scheming a perfect plan: to get pregnant and take the man away from his wife, who was already burdened with two children and a routine that consumed her. She, the mother, when discovering her husband's audacity in dividing his time between two homes, felt how the fear of losing him pierced her chest. It wasn't the money she feared losing; it was him. She, the mother, was a woman of flesh and blood, eternally in love and ruthlessly obsessed with her husband. She, the other woman, was neither younger nor older than the mother, but she had something that the mother lacked due to her devotion to the church: an audacious boldness and a history of men, men that the mother wouldn't even dare look at with the corner of her eye. She, the mother, used all her physical attributes to attract her husband and take him away from the other woman, even resorting to black magic. But that man was so enthralled with the other woman, that instead of drawing him closer, it pushed him further away. Not only did the man start sleeping at the other woman's house during the week, but also on weekends, awakening in the mother an existential bitterness, which she unjustly took out on her two children. But the opportunity for the story of *one stick* and *two homes* to change, presented itself one morning at her door, in the form of a milkman.

In desperation, the mother made a decision that would change the course of their lives. After her two sons had gone to school, she began inviting the *milkman* into her house, a fifteen year old man who abandoned school to sell milk door-to-door. The *milkman* was so poor that he looked like a *preñador*. The flirting took over two months before she managed to get him inside her—longer than she expected, as he was not accustomed to engaging with married women with children, and she was not accustomed to cheating on her husband. But one deposit of milk was all it took to get her pregnant.

When she told her husband that she was pregnant, he started to spend more time at the house, but during her pregnancy, there were rumors about the milkman and the *mother*—rumors that, of course, never got to her but to him. He confronted her, but mimicking her favorite mexican actresses, she strongly denied it all.

When Lincoln was born, his father held him in his arms and rejected him, feeling deep inside that he was not his son. The father looked for the milkman, and when he confronted him, the milkman's father burst into hearty laughter, asserting with a hint of disappointment that his son was far too foolish to seduce such a stunning woman, let alone get her pregnant. He licked his lips in front of his wife—the milkman's mother—while his thoughts wandered to the mother of his unknown grandchild.

Lincoln's father named the baby *Pastor* just to remind himself, every day, that he was an *'impostor.'* That was the first and last time that he held him in his arms.

Pastor grew into a bewildered child, unloved by his father for reasons unknown and visibly neglected by his own mother, whose adoration for her husband was unmistakable. The confusion and absence of affection made him sensitive, often shedding tears without cause and wrestling with a persistent sense of loneliness. To escape reality, Pastor turned to novels and movies. Hollywood films became his refuge, transporting him to idyllic two-story homes with loving families and fully stocked fridges. In those movies, food was always abundant, fathers were friendly, and mothers were caring. Lacking friends and resenting the company of other children who taunted him, Pastor carried with shame a set of delicate mannerisms, constantly facing ridicule wherever his legs took him.

At school, his classmates would drag him to the bathroom, strip him of his clothes, and force him to walk across the courtyard wearing

nothing but his underwear. Everyone laughed—
even the teachers, steeped in machismo. Silently
holding back his tears, he found himself wishing
to be paralyzed, longing to escape the burden of
walking. At home, his father—who was not his
father—watched him with disdain, and unable
to control his anger, would lock him for hours
in a wooden box. There, Pastor not only learned
to endure but also discovered the magic of
daydreaming until he drifted into a deep sleep.
One of those times, he dreamed that God, in His
massive presence, appeared atop his father's
desk. Confronting him about the mistreatment
of his son, God kicked him hard in the face.
Inside his box, still asleep, Pastor *laughed*.

In his darkest and most twisted thoughts,
Pastor wished for his father's death. Afterwards,
burdened with guilt, he sought forgiveness
from God, but the thoughts always returned in
a vicious circle of torment. Until one day, he
realized that his desire would never be fulfilled,
so he began to indulge in imagining how he
would kill him himself: perhaps with a kitchen
knife. But frightened by his own thoughts, he
ran to the church. Kneeling before the village
priest, he confessed with a trembling voice. The
priest, devout and wise, sternly warned him
that if he were to commit such a horrific act, he
would be condemned to spend the rest of his
days in prison and would never, ever enter the
kingdom of heaven. Pastor reflected, and with

the cold logic of a child clinging to a dream, he abandoned those diabolical thoughts.

At the age of twelve, driven by his father's irritation, who hated seeing him at home, Pastor found a job at a vegetable shop. Every Friday at two in the morning, he and his colleagues — men three times his age — loaded trucks with vegetables to export to the United States.

Before the truck departed, Pastor would always say goodbye to the vegetables with nostalgia, giving them names he invented himself. As he made his way home, he thought about the benefits of being a vegetable and the disadvantages of being a human.

One Thursday at midnight, at fourteen years old, with his legs bruised from his father's lashes for forgetting to stock the freezer with bags of water to avoid the unnecessary expense of buying ice to cool the sodas of the day, Pastor sat on his bed staring out the window, remembering the sermon from the priest who claimed that God was perfect, that He placed us in the best mommy's and daddy's belly in the world. Pastor, filled with anger and frustration, knew those words were lies.

The next day, he hid among the vegetables in the truck, and as the engine roared, he knew he was finally escaping from a life that, despite being his, did not belong to him.

WELCOME TO NEW YORK

"New York is New York, but Manhattan is more New York than New York. " Me

Lincoln was almost twenty years old. He wasn't as beautiful as a swan nor as ugly as a duck, but he had something special, something still untouchable. Like every winter, the snow fell, and Lincoln ran. It didn't matter where he went, time always seemed to catch up with him.

Manhattan was vast, magnificent, a city of ancient secrets and unrelenting energy. Its skyscrapers loomed with a wisdom and hunger of their own, towering over him like giants. In their shadows, Lincoln was small, brand new, and barely noticeable—a boy with nothing but big dreams and worn-out shoes, running just to keep from being swallowed whole.

Undocumented, he survived with two jobs. By day, he dressed up as Spider-Man, entertaining tourists in Times Square. Each time proving to himself he wasn't enough—too skinny, too small, too Latino, too poor. When the worn superhero suit was off, he worked his ass off as a busboy at a nightclub in Hell's Kitchen—a place where everyone with no home in the world belongs. Far from the heroics he played out in *Times Square* and cleaning Americans' *shit* at the nightclub, he loved New York without knowing why. The truth was, he hadn't even known it existed.

———

The night was cold and tinted with sparkly pink-blue hues outside, while inside, an unrelenting summer embraced everything. The air grew dense as if the entire space held its breath in unison. And there he was, Derrick Passeri. Among the crowd of *gay* men, Derrick wasn't one to blend in; he stood out with his stereotypical beauty, worthy of a magazine cover or iconic Hollywood movies. With his blond locks, a sharp diamond-shaped jawline, and a body sculpted by steroids and the gods he didn't believe in, he approached the bar. At the other side of the bar, Lincoln was cutting limes behind the counter, when he caught sight of Derrick Passeri's careful smile in response to a joke no one would ever remember but whose face Lincoln could never forget. Captivated, he found himself memorizing every feature of the beautiful man. Lost in the moment, Lincoln accidentally nicked his finger as he sliced the lime, the fruit slipping from the cutting board. A thin line of red traced his pale skin, but Derrick was the only one who noticed, offering a soft, knowing, mischievous smile as he rolled his eyes before turning away.

A week later, through coincidences no one would dare to explain, Lincoln found him smoking a cigarette, standing barefoot, clad in slightly damp blue jeans and a white tank top, as he leaned against the handrail outside his door. Lincoln, a shy and insecure creature, stared, but the thing with staring is that it confuses the one being stared at, not Derrick. He knew the effect he had on people, especially individuals like Lincoln. *Bungalow* was a rescued cat standing by the closed door, staring at Derrick. Lincoln went on to explain that the cat was left in his house by a friend; he lied to get his attention, but Derrick couldn't care less.

"Are you a cat person?" Lincoln grabbed the cat as he asked.

Derrick looked him in the eye. More than annoyed, he wondered what good he could get from engaging in a conversation with him.

"Your mother never taught you *not* to talk to strangers?" Derrick asked.

Lincoln never felt that he had one, and the pain across his face was enough to know half of his history. An uncomfortable silence followed the inconvenience of the wrong question at the right time.

"Are you a personal trainer?" Lincoln asked, quickly swifted from discomfort to joy, showing off a genuine spark of interest in his eyes.

19

It's been known across ages that gay men would use this question as a way to get a man's attention, and Lincoln, at his young age, was not the exception.

Derrick examined his small frame, forgetting the very beginning of his own physical transformation. He concluded that Lincoln was not interested in getting a better physique, but getting his attention.

"Why, are you looking for one?" Derrick asked.

"Yes, been looking around."

"You can't afford me," Derrick said as he put out the cigarette by stepping on it. The words stung more than Derrick could ever know.

Lincoln sensed a deeper meaning behind them, one Derrick likely hadn't intended—and in that, he was wrong.

Derrick turned and started to walk away from a scene that he wouldn't benefit from, only to discover that water was running out of the neighboring apartment. He ran into the apartment like a bullet. Lincoln followed him.

Derrick was an enigma to most, a solitary figure navigating the murky waters of life with a heavy heart and a mind clouded by bitterness. His days were painted with shades of darkness, a canvas tainted by the injustices he endured and the drugs he used to numb the pain. He wasn't one for making friends or keeping up with the latest trends, and you wouldn't catch him dead on social media, *not* with the skeletons lurking in his closet. He also harbored a strong aversion towards individuals with excess weight, a sentiment that extended to his grandmother, Sofia, whose imposing physical presence in her youth mirrored her larger-than-life personality. Despite her declarations of affection, her affectionate gestures often felt suffocating and unsettling to him. At the tender age of eight, Derrick gathered the courage to confront Sofia about his father, a question his mother had evaded. With gentle strokes through his blond locks, Sofia disclosed a harsh truth:

"Even your own mother didn't know who your father is. All the things you learn in an orgy. That's how slutty your mother was," she concluded.

Derrick's understanding of adult concepts came prematurely, and among them was the meaning of "*orgy*." It was a lesson learned far too early, imprinting upon him a knowledge of carnal indulgence before he was equipped to comprehend its complexities or consequences.

As Derrick expected, upon entering the neighboring apartment, he went straight to the bathroom, where the overflowing bathtub cradled an old man's lifeless body within its porcelain confines. The old man, with his weathered features and tired eyes, bore the marks of a life hard-lived, yet his stillness spoke of a journey nearing its end. At just 80 years old, he might have deemed himself too weary to continue.

Derrick, driven by desperation and adrenaline, pulled Old Clint from the water, his hands trembling as he began the rhythmic compressions of CPR. Despite his frantic efforts, the old man remained unresponsive. Lincoln, alarmed by the commotion, stepped forward to intervene, only to be met with a sudden blow that left a deep bruise etched upon his face. Fueled by a surge of anger and determination, Derrick unleashed his frustration on the bathroom tiles instead of Lincoln's youthful face, the sound of breaking ceramic mingling with the echoes of his desperation. For a fleeting moment, he glanced at Lincoln, who now stood in silent shock, cradling his cheek. A pang of regret stirred within Derrick—an emotion he wasn't accustomed to letting surface. He clenched his jaw, suppressing the urge to apologize, and redirected his focus back to Old Clint. Kneeling beside the lifeless man, Derrick resumed his efforts, counting each compression under his breath until, miraculously, the old man stirred back to life. Exhausted yet victorious, Derrick slumped back against the flooded bathroom floor, his heart pounding in his chest as he watched Old Clint slowly regain consciousness.

"Who are you?" Old Clint asked, looking at Lincoln's scared face, his voice tinged with confusion. Derrick, unable to resist the temptation to stir the pot, replied with a sly grin, "That's my boyfriend." The words hung in the air, laden with tension and defiance. It was a calculated move intended to unsettle Clint and assert Derrick's control. And while it may have achieved its desired effect at the moment, it would ultimately lead to their swift expulsion from Old Clint's apartment.

———

Old Clint and Derrick met on a rainy day when Derrick was taken into custody for a bad fight that concluded with his opponent in the hospital, nursing a couple of bruises and two missing teeth. It wasn't anything too serious, but his opponent, a flamboyant character with the spirit of Marilyn Monroe, exaggerated the whole situation and pressed charges. Derrick didn't utter a word in his defense, mainly because he was disgusted by his opponent's whole persona. He'd rather have gone to jail than listen to that cringy voice again. The incident occurred at a bar on 51st St., where Derrick and RedSaint were having cocktails. This bold little character in shiny clothes and makeup slipped his filthy fingers into RedSaint's drink and then sensually licked them while gazing at him with burning desire. RedSaint wasn't thrilled by the act, but it was Derrick who felt deeply disrespected. He grabbed RedSaint's drink and handed it back to the boy, asking him, rather nicely, to buy a new one for RedSaint. The boy strongly refused, claiming he was broke and only had enough for his *MetroCard* to get home. In the end, Derrick reluctantly covered the boy's medical bills,

23

paying $10,000 in damages. Additionally, he was sentenced to community service.

Clint was too old to be actively proactive. He used to be a proud American, energized by the sight of the flag. He could have happily died for his country in the war, but instead, he survived with no legs, only to realize that his country didn't care for him as much as he did for it. He was too young when all of this happened, and over time, the rage, the disappointment, and the loneliness turned him into a horrible person inside and out.

As part of his community service, Derrick's job was to ensure that Clint had fresh food in the fridge and a clean house to live in. The relationship between the two was fine, because whatever Clint had to say, Derrick didn't care about or pay attention to.

———

After being kicked out of Clint's apartment, Lincoln, with his face bruised, invited Derrick to his own place to tend to his broken knuckles. Derrick, who ignored the bruise stamped on Lincoln's face, hesitated. Lincoln's bathroom was smaller than the tiniest matchbox you could imagine. Even though Derrick was a New Yorker, he felt a sudden wave of claustrophobia as he stepped into that suspiciously narrow bathroom.

With trembling hands and more nerves than experience, Lincoln submerged Derrick's hand into the sink full of ice-cold water and ice cubes that cracked with contact. As his fingers sank into the water, Derrick lifted his gaze and found himself staring at Lincoln's face. The punch he had delivered was starting to leave its mark on his skin, a purple bruise that seemed to silently scream. Lincoln felt it, those intense blue eyes locked on him, and, as if they burned, he avoided returning the gaze. It wasn't from a lack of interest, but from an irrational fear. He feared that if he looked into Derrick's eyes, he might see his imperfections and read his insecurities. So, instead, he focused on what he had in front of him: Derrick's injured hand. He rubbed it with a tender clumsiness, trying to soothe the pain under the cold water. Suddenly, Derrick broke the silence. With an unexpected move, he placed his hands on Lincoln's face, holding it firmly but without harshness. Lincoln flinched, intimidated that Derrick might deliver another blow. Derrick began massaging the area where the punch had landed, trying to alleviate the swelling before the bruise settled in.

"Stay still," Derrick ordered, his voice more of a plea disguised as authority. Lincoln, as if his words were a spell, obeyed without questioning. He closed his eyes, allowing Derrick to continue, letting the pain settle as he gripped Derrick's strong forearm. There was nothing Derrick could ask of him that he wouldn't be willing to give.

Derrick's hand began to hurt, possibly from fractured knuckles. He gave up on massaging the bruise and took out a small bag of ketamine from his waist pouch, handing it to Lincoln.

"Make me a bump with this," Derrick said, handing him the bag and a tiny steel spoon. Lincoln took the bag without knowing what to do with it, examining it cautiously. He wasn't dumb, but he confused the contents with cocaine. Frowning, he asked, "What does this do?"

Derrick gave a half-smile. "It calms the pain."

Lincoln raised an eyebrow, questioning the answer without saying anything. That small action seemed to break the wall of ignorance that protected him from Derrick's truths.

"Do you want some?" Derrick asked, staring him directly in the eyes.

"No!" Lincoln replied, fearful of falling into what was written as forbidden.

Lincoln loaded the spoon with the powder, and Derrick exhaled deeply.

"Are you sure you don't want some?" Derrick asked as he prepared to inhale more ketamine through the other nostril.

Lincoln hesitated, but there was nothing in this world that Derrick could ask him to do that he wouldn't be willing to do. That look, which suspended itself in the air without gravity, marked the beginning of the end.

———

There are two types of people in the world: those like Derrick and those like Lincoln. Although these two types of people may seem opposites, they rarely mix. Not because they are completely different, but because they are one degree away from becoming the same.

The party was set with hundreds of men, and not because of the heat, they all decided not to wear t-shirts. Lincoln had been here more than any of its guests, probably not smelling fresh, mostly due to hard labor such as picking up the trash, transporting bottles and garnishes from the basement to the bars, and cleaning little pukes everywhere. Although that night he showered prior to his arrival. And, even if he wasn't smelling of sweet *Louis Vuitton* like Derrick, no one could say that he didn't look brand new. He naively dragged his value up to the ceiling but immediately dropped down when he realized that he didn't belong among these sorts of men, for instance, body size and money.

Derrick offered him an ecstasy pill, but he quickly rejected it. He knew what it was, and it reminded himself not to consume pills unless they were Tylenol.

"Why not?" Derrick asked.

"It's not my thing," Lincoln replied.

"It's not my thing either," Derrick shot back as he put the ecstasy pill in Lincoln's mouth. Lincoln took it out of his mouth, held it in his hands, and stared at him, upset.

"What?" Derrick asked, annoyed. Lincoln didn't answer, but his scary look was everything.

"Take it; everyone in here took one of these," Derrick said, pushing him to take the pill.

"I'll get a drink," Lincoln retorted.

"No one in here is drinking," Derrick said.

Lincoln started to look around the people, but Derrick grabbed his chin, making him look at him into his blue eyes. "I said no one is drinking alcohol," he added, "You either take it or *fucking* go home, do you understand?" Derrick concluded, firmly.

"And what do I get?" He asked with unnatural confidence. Derrick almost burst laughing, not because the remark was funny but because of the quirky response,

"A picture of us," Lincoln proposed before Derrick got the chance to say something.

"What?" Derrick asked, wondering if he heard well, "A picture of us, you said?"

Lincoln's eyes stayed fixed on Derrick as his life depended on it.

"Don't take this the wrong way, but I wouldn't take a picture with me; if I were you," he said, watching Lincoln shrink to the size of a peanut. "Are you taking the damn pill or not?" He added, frustrated in a firm tone.

Lincoln, without thinking, swallowed the pill, feeling both the pill and Derrick's indifference settle heavily in his guts. He regretted it at once.

What he knew so far about drugs is that most people lose it all, and some others turn into unrecognizable humans, and some others live on the streets after losing it all and becoming unrecognizable people.

Lincoln felt fear, but Derrick's satisfied smile across his face convinced him that everything was going to be just fine. While Derrick smiled not because he was happy, but because he had better plans for the night and for the boy, poor thing.

The first effect that manifested in Lincoln's small frame was the urgency to use the toilet, "I need the bathroom," He said, demanding to be walked there.

"You work here. You know where it is." Derrick shot back.

Lincoln could've taken this behavior as mean, but he was so infatuated with Derrick that he decided not to notice it, so he went to the bathroom by himself with heavy feet, a dizziness that prevented him from walking straight, and the need to poop. Arriving at the bathroom, he felt the need to puke, but a skinny black girl in white, with a dick between her legs, said "Honey, puke here," walking him to the garbage tank. Lincoln tried to puke, but nothing came out.

"Did you just take a pill?" she asked.

Lincoln nodded.

"No puking at the club, dear. You don't puke, and you don't poop in the club, no, no, no," she said as she walked him towards the sink, "drink water, so it will go down," she opened the faucet and pressed his head down for him to drink water straight from the faucet. "You here with friends, dear?" She asked.

"My boyfriend," Lincoln replied as water was getting into his mouth.

"And, where the *fuck* is your boyfriend?"

"Outside," He replied.

"What did you take?"

"A pill."

"A pill of what?" She challenged him.

"A pill!" He shot back. She realized that he was younger and more naive that she expected.

"How old are you?"

"Twenty-one," He lied.

"Twenty-one, and you took a pill and you have no idea what it is?"

"My boyfriend gave it to me." He said, barely audibly.

"Where's he that he's not here, taking care of you?"

"Stop, just stop for one second" Lincoln asked her as he closed his eyes, pulled his hair back facing to the ceiling, and started controlling his breathing. He felt a surge of energy raising from his feet and turned towards the mirror to notice that he was sweating like a pig. In his reflection something had drastically changed, but he was too new to this to knew what it was.

She studied him and immediately knew. "Is this your first time?" she asked, remembering her first time taking the *ecstasy* almost twenty years ago when she was fifteen. Back then, the feeling of getting high was worth living. Now, she silently and hypocritically regretted it.

Lincoln smiled, welcoming this new ascending energy. He nodded as a thankful gesture to her for taking care of him, and then, started to walk away.

"Don't fall for him," She said, grabbing his arm and feeling deeply sorry for him. "He's *not* worth it."

"You don't know him." Lincoln shot back, and left.

———

Lincoln woke up hanging from a sling in the arms of a stranger who used his body to satisfy what, on a daily basis, would get off with pornography on the internet. The pulsating rhythm of techno music cocooned the room in a cryptic atmosphere, like announcing a pending deadly pleasure in someone's tragedy. Naturally cloaked in darkness, the place seemed as if it had been born in the shadows. An aged, solitary red exit sign, mounted high on the wall, cast a faint glow that barely reached their faces but not their rotten souls. It almost felt criminal to be in that place. Six men, visibly high on crystal meth, surrounded Lincoln, jerking their wiener as each waited silently, impatient for their turn. A part of Lincoln died on the dance floor, and the other one struggled to survive at the hands of these men. In his confusion, he desperately searched for Derrick's face, but all he could find were ugly faces and his own reflection in the mirror on the ceiling.

Red Saint, who was in possession of Lincoln, had his eyes fixed on him, making Lincoln's pain part of his own pleasure. Suddenly, he cast his gaze toward Derrick, who was seated six feet away, lacking entertainment. Red Saint dismounted Lincoln and walked towards him.

"What's wrong?" Red Saint asked, annoyed.

Derrick rose and walked off.

Red Saint followed him.

Derrick emerged from the warehouse, hastily pulling on his T-shirt as he approached his Jeep. Despite the early hour, the sunlight bore down intensely, mimicking the midday heat.

"You can't be done. You haven't started yet."

"I had fun." Derrick lied.

"Bullshit...you haven't even touched the kid." Red Saint retorted.

"Not my type," Derrick responded.

"You made me fuck that kid, and now he's not your *fucking* type." Red Saint challenged him as Derrick climbed into his jeep.

"Drop it," Derrick said firmly as he put on his high-end aviator sunglasses, ignited the engine, and their eyes locked.

"You're a *fucking* asshole," Red Saint spat out, the veins in his face pulsating with anger as his hand shot towards Derrick's throat.

Without a word, Derrick made a swift exit, and left home, where he filled the apartment with strangers from Grindr and Scruff, hosting an orgy and indulging in drugs, while the music set the mood. As night fell, the cold winter crept through the gaps in the old air conditioner. While covering it with a blanket, he noticed the first snowfall outside the window. A thought invaded his mind and wouldn't leave: Lincoln.

At midnight, the sound of the door opening pulled him from his troubled thoughts. It was RedSaint, entering with more men, his dominant energy filling the space like a cold gust. Derrick watched him approach, with his usual arrogance, as the other men scattered around the apartment.

"What happened to the kid?" Derrick asked, not remembering his name, trying to sound indifferent, but something in his tone gave him away.

RedSaint smirked mockingly, clearly high.

"Why do you care?"

"Where did you leave him?"

"Why don't you fix us a dose instead, you're unbearable."

"I'm not joking, Red. Where did you leave him?" Derrick said through gritted teeth, gripping his arm tightly.

RedSaint pushed him, feeling threatened.

"Hey!" one of the friends intervened, stopping the fight. "We left him at the usual spot," he confessed.

"At the train station, in the park, at the bus stop, by the pier... where's the usual spot?" Derrick yelled, his voice rising above the chaos of the music and the laughter of the men.

He drove to Brooklyn, to a desolate area where warehouses and trees stood tall in a lonely and eerie neighborhood. That night, the snow fell heavily, creating an enchanting purple atmosphere. In the haze, he found Lincoln at an old bus stop, wrapped in a wool blanket. His head looked dead on top of a garbage bag. He was sitting on a bench with his right temple pressed against the cold metal. Derrick cautiously approached, his instinct prompting him to check for signs of life. A broad, relieved smile appeared as he discerned Lincoln's steady breaths. However, his joy faded when he observed Lincoln's face adhered to the cold metal surface. With warm breath against the affected area, Derrick attempted to gently free Lincoln's head from its icy grip.

Derrick decided not to take Lincoln to the apartment he shared with RedSaint. Instead, he drove to his grandmother's house, Sofía Passeri. Sofía was an older woman who lived comfortably thanks to the success of her YouTube channel, where she told fictional stories of her life, giving advice about all the things she didn't do. Derrick placed Lincoln in his old teenage bedroom.

Sofía, worried, tried to clean and take care of Lincoln, but when she asked about him, Derrick was evasive. When Sofía suggested calling the police, he kicked her out of the room, thanking her for her help, but brusquely. Sofía left, concerned about the possible consequences.

In the solitude of the room, Derrick removed the blanket covering Lincoln, revealing a torso marked with bruises—clear signs of abuse. He took a deep breath, a wave of guilt washing over him. Not unfamiliar with such experiences, he prepared a bathtub with hot water, gently lowering both his body and Lincoln's into it, hoping to ease the pain that, in his current state, Lincoln couldn't even feel. That night, Derrick couldn't sleep. And Lincoln didn't wake up.

Any other day, in his own bed, Lincoln would have woken early with the sun on his face. But in Derrick's dim room, the sun didn't reach him.

By 2:10 p.m., Sofia entered with hot soup, but an unpleasant odor stopped her in her tracks. Following the smell, she approached Derrick's bed, where Lincoln lay motionless. She peeled back the sheets, recoiling at what she saw—soiled bedding and streaks of blood. Shocked, she screamed, a sound she hadn't made since Derrick was a baby.

The scream jolted Lincoln awake. His eyes widened in horror as he realized the extent of his humiliation. In a panic, he rolled up the sheets and bolted to the bathroom, leaving Sofia standing there, horrified and unsure if the blood was serious. Lincoln locked himself in the bathroom for over two hours, battling relentless diarrhea, dehydration. He managed to find medicine in Derrick's cabinet, which helped stabilize him. Afterward, he washed the bloody sheets in the bathtub, wringing them out with trembling hands. When he finally emerged, pale and weak, his eyes fell on a note left by Derrick on the nightstand: "I DON T LIVE HERE. LEAVE AND DO NOT STEAL A THING."

Lincoln's expression shifted from disappointment to quiet resolve. Taking a pen, he scrawled a response on the back of the paper: "CALL ME, LINCOLN. I LOVE YOU." He added his phone number with a small, hopeful heart.

Before leaving, he rummaged through the closet for something warm and slipped on a hoodie. He closed the door behind him softly, leaving Sofia's house unnoticed. Instead of heading home, Lincoln went straight to his writing class, despite his worsening condition. The effects of the previous night weighed heavily on him. The aftermath of being sexually assaulted was physically brutal—fissures around the anus made every trip to the bathroom agonizing, and the frequent diarrhea drained his body, leaving him dehydrated and weak. On top of that, the drugs he had ingested dulled his appetite and exacerbated a depression he didn't even realize had taken root.

When Lincoln finally arrived at class, late as usual, his professor, Linda Smirnoff, glared at him with a mixture of irritation and curiosity. Without preamble, she demanded, "Read your poetry."

Lincoln, slumped in the back row, shook his head respectfully. "I can't," he murmured.

Linda's lips tightened in offense. "If you're not going to participate, then leave," she snapped.

Weary and resigned, Lincoln rose from his seat. He hadn't written anything for class and lacked the strength to argue. As he reached the door, Linda addressed the rest of the room, her tone sharp. "Poetry is like a diary written for strangers to read."

Something in her words stopped him. Slowly, he turned back and walked toward her desk, his footsteps deliberate. Without looking at anyone, but her, while reciting his verses.

The Beast took me by surprise,
dragged me naked into the night
where the moonlight stood
until midnight.

A dream or a nightmare—
what's the difference,
if I've seen it all?

Pleasure or pain—
what's the difference,
if I've felt it all?

Red from my love.
Red from my own blood.

Tell me,
what's the difference between
the red from my own love
and the red from my own blood,
if I have lost it all?

Where are you,
that I can't find you?

Where are you?
And don't say "somewhere,"
because Somewhere could be here,
Somewhere could be there,
Somewhere could be anywhere.

The Beast took me by surprise,
dragged me naked into the night.

Linda tried to hide her admiration. For a moment, her stern eyes softened, caught by the raw beauty of the poem Lincoln had just recited. As he finished, his face was so close to hers that he could smell her breath, even though her mouth was closed. In an impulsive and defiant gesture, he kissed her on the lips, leaving the entire class in stunned silence. But then, urgency overtook him. He bolted to the bathroom, and as he sat on the toilet, his body gave way. Moments later, he collapsed unconscious onto the cold floor. When he woke up, he was lying on a stretcher in the school's emergency room, an IV dripping fluid into his arm. The soft tapping of the IV was the only sound breaking the sterile silence of the room. A doctor looked at him with concern, peppering him with questions about his condition. Avoiding any incriminating details, Lincoln weakly responded:

"Chronic diarrhea..."

Linda visited Lincoln in the hospital, a mix of fascination and curiosity in her expression. She leaned toward him, praising his poem with words that seemed both sincere and measured. However, she was taken aback to learn that the poem hadn't been written beforehand but had been improvised in the heat of the moment.

"You should write it down before you forget it," she suggested, pulling a notebook and pen from her bag.

Lincoln squinted at her, weakened but with a sly glimmer in his eyes that peeked through the veil of his pain.

"I'll write the poem if you hire me as your assistant at The New Yorker."

Linda, though impressed by his audacity, raised an eybrow as she weighed his proposition. It wasn't the first time Lincoln had asked her for a job as her assistant. On multiple occasions, Linda had explained that he wasn't ready for the position. But she also knew the harsh reality of Lincoln's life: scraping by on meager tips earned while entertaining tourists in *Times Square* in a ridiculous Spider-Man costume. She was well aware of his dream to escape poverty. However, she also recognized the shortcomings in his writing and his precarious immigration status. His work, while promising, was littered with overblown vocabulary, clearly plucked from a dictionary in a desperate bid to impress. It was ornate but hollow; complex yet disconnected from a deeper truth. His writing lacked the maturity that only lived experience could provide.

"You can't write about the world if you haven't lived it, Lincoln," she had once told him, with the conviction of someone who believed in potential only half-fulfilled.

In response to his attempt at blackmail, Linda put her notebook and pen away, maintaining an air of distant professionalism. The poem, titled *'The Black Night and the Red of My Own Blood,'* faded from Lincoln's memory, like a dream that vanishes upon waking. And though Linda would never admit it, deep down she regretted not finding a way to preserve that poem.

Even if Lincoln did not write the poem; he did practice a speech of all the things he wanted to say to the man who saved him and then abandoned him.

———

The following Friday, Lincoln arrived at the nightclub where he worked, trying to appear normal. From the moment he walked through the door, he felt the unwavering gaze of his boss fixed on him. She was a confident Latina woman in her mid-40s, known for her strong personality and sharp business acumen. She immediately called him into her office.

"Close the door," she ordered without preamble.

Lincoln, nervous, obeyed.

"We need to talk about what happened last weekend," she began, lighting a cigarette—a habit she reserved only for moments of stress.

"What happened?" Lincoln asked, trying to sound innocent, though something inside him was beginning to twist.

"I saw you dancing on the dance floor, intoxicated—who knows on what—instead of doing your job," she said, her gaze a mix of disappointment and weariness.

"That's not true," Lincoln quickly retorted, but his tone betrayed him.

"Oh, isn't it?" she replied, raising an eyebrow and tapping on her phone. She turned the screen toward him.

In the video, Lincoln appeared moving erratically, sweating, his eyes glazed as he danced on the floor. Another clip showed him stumbling toward the bathroom, where a Black woman helped him vomit into a trash can before two men dragged him out of the club, completely unconscious.

Lincoln swallowed hard. He had no response. The images were undeniable.

"Who are those men?" she asked, her eyes drilling into him, trying to decipher the truth.

"They're my friends," he replied unconvincingly, staring at the floor.

"Your friends?" she repeated sarcastically, letting out a disbelieving laugh. "Those are not your friends."

"Yes, they are," Lincoln insisted, but his voice wavered.

She studied him for a moment, as if trying to read between the lines. "Did they drug you?" she asked, lowering her voice, this time with genuine concern.

"No!" Lincoln answered immediately, his tone firm, almost defiant.

She stared at him, trying to detect any cracks in his response. She knew he was lying but understood she wouldn't get more out of him.

"Listen, Lincoln, I can't keep you here. You're fired," she said finally, her tone a mix of frustration and disappointment.

His eyes welled with tears. Although he protested her decision, she was resolute.

41

It was too early to go home and too late to head to work in Times Square, so, with nothing else to do, Lincoln decided to stay, trying to drown his frustration with cocktails the bartender offered him on the house.

As the night progressed, his intoxication deepened, and his thoughts began to wander to the go-go dancers gleaming on the cubes. Watching them, he wondered if someone as perfect as they were could ever be fired. He raised his glass in an ironic toast to the mothers of those men who had made them so beautiful.

A bandaged hand rested on the bar next to Lincoln. Intrigued and drunk, Lincoln stared at it, trying to connect the image to a memory. When he looked up, he recognized the beautiful face and smiled.

"Hi!" he said with excessive confidence, thanks to the alcohol.

Derrick, who had initially been in a good mood, frowned when he recognized him.

"Your hand... it looks better," Lincoln commented, reaching out to touch it. Derrick instinctively pulled it away, avoiding contact.

"Don't you remember me?" Lincoln asked, confused by his reaction.

Before Derrick could respond, RedSaint's commanding voice interrupted the scene.

"I'd be surprised if your own mother remembers you," he said, placing his massive frame in front of Lincoln, caricaturing the young man's slender figure.

If he hadn't been drunk, Lincoln would have run to the bathroom to cry, but instead, he stopped to look at the bulging veins in RedSaint's arms, silently wondering what would happen if they suddenly burst.

"Why aren't you unclogging the toilets?" RedSaint added with a seriousness that seemed out of place on his face.

Humiliated, Lincoln searched for Derrick's gaze, but Derrick's attention was elsewhere, lost in the crowd.

Lincoln grabbed his empty glass and, ashamed, began to walk away. As he glanced back at Derrick, their eyes met briefly, and Derrick responded by rolling his eyes in contempt.

When the party reached its climax and all the drugs took effect, Lincoln, who had been watching Derrick from the shadows, gathered the courage to approach when he noticed RedSaint stepping away from the impenetrable circle of muscular, attractive men.

"Hi!" Lincoln said, touching Derrick's bare shoulder, now with a shaky confidence born of his desperation to connect.

Derrick turned abruptly, brushing Lincoln's hand away without touching it.

"Who's this?" one of the men asked, a muscular guy radiating arrogance.

"Nobody," Derrick replied indifferently, turning back to his group and leaving Lincoln standing there, feeling the weight of humiliation.

Confused, Lincoln stepped back, his cheeks burning as he tried to hide his embarrassment.

He returned to the bar, his mind swirling with questions and excuses to justify Derrick's behavior: "Maybe he felt uncomfortable in front of his friends... Maybe he didn't want them to see him with me... Maybe I was too forward..." he thought, his eyes fixed on the empty glass in front of him. Fighting back tears, Lincoln raised his hand to order another cocktail, trying to drown the searing feeling of rejection that consumed him. But he couldn't tear his gaze away from Derrick, who kept laughing with his group of friends as if nothing had happened, his presence radiating a mix of magnetism and cruelty. The bar became Lincoln's temporary refuge, but his heart remained on the dance floor, trapped in a tangle of unrequited desires. Suddenly, moving with the urgency of someone who didn't want to be seen, Derrick, his bandaged hand leading the way, grabbed Lincoln by the arm and pulled him toward a staircase that descended into the dark room.

The dark room was a space where the music reverberated more intensely, but there were no lights, plunging the area into total darkness. Derrick, with determination, pinned Lincoln against a wall, gripping his neck with his bandaged hand.

"Don't look at me. Don't talk to me. Don't follow me," Derrick ordered, his face barely illuminated by a faint flicker of blue and red light.

Before Lincoln could respond, Derrick pulled out a *Euphorix* pill and, with an almost feral intensity, shoved it into Lincoln's mouth. Then he kissed him, flooding his mouth with saliva to ensure he swallowed it.

"When can I see you?" Lincoln asked desperately, clutching Derrick's arm as if it were his last hope.

Derrick looked at him with a mix of amusement and caution, his lips curling into an enigmatic smile.

"Be very careful. I'm a dangerous drug for someone like you."

"You're a dangerous drug for anyone," Lincoln replied with unexpected audacity.

Derrick pressed his lips together, staring at him intently.

"Exactly."

"So, when can I see you?"

"I'm not interested."

Derrick started to leave, but Lincoln grabbed his arm tightly.

"Let me prove you're wrong," Lincoln insisted, his pleading eyes shining in the darkness.

Derrick stepped closer to him, his severe expression hardening further.

"The next time you bother me, I'll gouge your eyes out," Derrick concluded, his tone sharp and final, leaving no room for further discussion.

Though disappointed, Lincoln showed no fear. His fingers, which had clung tightly to Derrick's arm, slowly loosened until they let go completely. Derrick turned and walked away, leaving Lincoln standing there, motionless, feeling his heart shatter into pieces.

As he emerged from the dark room, Lincoln looked around and quickly realized the problem wasn't that Derrick didn't like him. It was that Derrick didn't like his lanky arms or his shapeless body. Although his face wasn't magazine-worthy, it possessed an exotic quality that had clearly piqued Derrick's interest. Otherwise, Derrick wouldn't have invited him out, much less saved him from that dark night. Standing at the foot of that animal kingdom that had rejected him, Lincoln made a decision that would change the course of his days.

———

After Derrick rejected him, Lincoln became self-conscious about his body. Everywhere his eyes landed, that was all he could focus on. He recognized, perhaps more acutely than 80% of the gay population, that achieving success as a gay man often hinged on possessing an attractive physique. It appeared that the mindset and methods to achieve this goal were irrelevant. For a considerable period, he had chosen to feign ignorance, avoiding any contact with a gym due to his inherent laziness. However, the reality became painfully clear. He needed to transform himself into something more akin to Derrick and less like his true self. However, Santiago, his cosplay mate from Times Square, was a striking figure. At just 23 years old, his dark skin and Greek-like symmetry made it nearly impossible to look away. Like Lincoln, he donned a Spider-

Man costume every day to entertain tourists. Yet, while Lincoln struggled to scrape by, Santiago excelled, effortlessly standing out and filling his pockets with dollar bills by the end of each day. On more than one occasion, Santiago had tried to drag Lincoln to the gym, extolling its benefits, but Lincoln always responded with a tired tone, "Tomorrow." The day he finally asked for help, Santiago, without question, took him to his gym. It wasn't the most expensive, but it wasn't the cheapest either. There, the receptionist charged $40 for a day of training, flatly refusing to grant him a free pass. To Lincoln, $40 represented an entire day of work. While a gym membership might be considered a luxury by many, for others, like Derrick and Lincoln, it was an absolute necessity. For Derrick, the gym was a practical means to channel his tensions, even if it didn't always work. For Lincoln, it represented the only way to become one of Derrick's many tensions. But nothing in New York is free. If your aspirations are greater than your wallet's reach, you end up cleaning bathrooms in exchange for a membership. In his stubbornness and desperation, Lincoln offered his cleaning services in exchange for a membership and a small salary. However, as an undocumented immigrant, he was only offered the membership. Santiago said nothing, but his face reflected a mix of pity and frustration, as if the rejection hurt him more than it did his friend.

As he emerged from the dark room, Lincoln looked around and quickly realized the problem wasn't that Derrick didn't like him. It was that Derrick didn't like his lanky arms or his shapeless body. Although his face wasn't magazine-worthy, it possessed an exotic quality that had clearly piqued Derrick's interest. Otherwise, Derrick wouldn't have invited him out, much less saved him from that dark night. Standing at the foot of that animal kingdom that had rejected him, Lincoln made a decision that would change the course of his days.

———

After Derrick rejected him, Lincoln became self-conscious about his body. Everywhere his eyes landed, that was all he could focus on. He recognized, perhaps more acutely than 80% of the gay population, that achieving success as a gay man often hinged on possessing an attractive physique. It appeared that the mindset and methods to achieve this goal were irrelevant. For a considerable period, he had chosen to feign ignorance, avoiding any contact with a gym due to his inherent laziness. However, the reality became painfully clear. He needed to transform himself into something more akin to Derrick and less like his true self. However, Santiago, his cosplay mate from Times Square, was a striking figure. At just 23 years old, his dark skin and Greek-like symmetry made it nearly impossible to look away. Like Lincoln, he donned a Spider-Man costume every day to entertain tourists. Yet, while Lincoln struggled to scrape by, Santiago excelled, effortlessly standing out and filling his pockets with dollar bills by the end of each day. On more than one occasion, Santiago had tried to drag Lincoln to the gym, extolling its benefits, but Lincoln always responded with a tired tone, "Tomorrow." The day he finally asked for help, Santiago, without question, took him to his gym. It wasn't the most expensive, but it wasn't the cheapest either. There, the receptionist charged $40 for a day of training, flatly refusing to grant him a free pass. To Lincoln, $40 represented an entire day of work. While a gym membership might be considered a luxury by many, for others, like Derrick and Lincoln, it was an absolute necessity. For Derrick, the gym was a practical means to channel his tensions, even if it didn't always work. For Lincoln, it represented the only way to become one of Derrick's many tensions. But nothing in New York is free. If your aspirations are greater than your wallet's reach, you end up cleaning bathrooms in exchange for a membership. In his stubbornness and desperation, Lincoln offered his cleaning services in exchange for a membership and a small salary. However, as an undocumented immigrant, he was only offered the membership. Santiago said nothing, but his face reflected a mix of pity and frustration, as if the rejection hurt him more than it did his friend.

"When you gain some weight, you'll feel more motivated," Santiago said with a forced smile, trying to encourage him, "and your tips will cover the membership." Additionally, Santiago offered Lincoln personalized training and a steroid cycle to accelerate his growth process. The day after the first intramuscular injection, Lincoln froze in front of the bathroom mirror. His eyes caught something he had never seen before: a distinct line emerging at the bottom of his flat chest—the very same chest that had tormented him every time he looked at it. For a moment, the world stopped. A tingling sensation, a mix of disbelief and hope, coursed through his body. That small, almost insignificant change was a turning point for him. That day, he promised himself he wouldn't stop for anything or anyone.

The gym's bathrooms sparkled, the mirrors gleamed, and the floors remained spotless. Lincoln's commitment yielded remarkable results, transforming him from a no-salary earner to a respectable $15-an-hour income. While not a fortune, when combined with his cosplay earnings, it allowed him to lead a more comfortable life. Unexpectedly, he found himself browsing Amazon for a larger-sized Spider-Man outfit to accommodate the newfound development in his legs. However, one fateful day, heavy rain engulfed New York City, and Derrick, searching for a place to work out, had no choice but to purchase a day pass for the nearest gym. Like clockwork, before starting his workout, Derrick followed his daily routine of using the bathroom. Unintentionally, he entered a stall occupied by a kneeling Lincoln, cleaning the toilet. Their eyes locked, and Derrick hastily locked himself in the adjacent stall. Lincoln remained frozen for a moment, then rose, removed his gloves, walked off, and never came back.

Santiago was not very happy with Lincoln quitting the job; he saw his friend putting so much effort into the cleaning that he couldn't help but feel disappointed. But Lincoln explained that cleaning toilets was not what he wanted to do, so Santiago let it go and supported his friend unknowingly. In fact, Santiago, who identified as heterosexual, didn't know that Lincoln, who identified as gay, was mentally involved with a man, and he was the reason that ruined it all.

After that uncomfortable encounter in the bathroom between Lincoln and Derrick, Lincoln returned to his full-time gig cosplaying as Spider-Man in *Times Square*. The money started rolling in, surpassing what he ever earned at the gym and even edging out Santiago, who naturally excelled in his field. Lincoln became a member of a decent gym for a low budget persona on the east side, refusing to relent in his pursuit of a bulkier physique. His fear of reverting to his once-skinny self was a closely guarded secret.

———

The eagerly awaited night finally arrived. Lincoln donned a pair of snug blue jeans and a plain white t-shirt, and in his new sneakers, he headed straight to the *gay* nightclub where Derrick had first introduced him to, for him, still an unknown world. As another Friday night unfolded, the nightclub was jam-packed and moist. New York City has been known for being the capital of the world, and the party crowd wouldn't say otherwise. Each shirtless man along the way was on a protein diet, and if they were to get paid for each workout they had done in their life, they all would have been millionaires, but most of them were living in bedrooms the size of a matchbox, filled with high-end apparel, and burdened with massive credit card debt that they wouldn't be able to pay back in a million years. However, they were dancing and getting artificially high levels of serotonin, as if that night were their last. On the inside, Lincoln felt like a chicken in the wrong coop, but on the outside, he could have been one of them.

The hours passed with no sign of Derrick. The music blended with the flashing lights, but for Lincoln, everything was beginning to fade into a haze of disappointment. Tired, he started to lose hope in the night. Unexpectedly, several men approached him. Some offered suggestive smiles, others, direct gestures aimed at grabbing his attention. But Lincoln chose to ignore them all. He knew that as soon as he gave his attention to someone else, Derrick would appear, and with that, his chance to regain their connection would vanish. So, he waited, determined to hold on to the place he had reserved for Derrick—if only in his mind. However, one of his admirers didn't seem to pick up on the subtle rejection. He danced too close, right behind Lincoln, at first without contact, as if he were simply following the rhythm of the music. But soon, the proximity grew. A stranger's hand slid softly along Lincoln's spine, drawing a line with the tip of a finger. Lincoln tensed but didn't move. The hand returned—this time, there were two—applying gentle pressure to his waist, making him hold his breath. The stranger moved closer, leaning in until his chin rested on the back of Lincoln's neck. Then he inhaled deeply, as if trying to capture the scent of his skin. Lincoln closed his eyes, a shiver running through him as his mind struggled to process what was happening. Then, something familiar emerged: a scent he recognized, one he had felt before, one that had enveloped him like a refuge. Out of the corner of his eye, Lincoln saw a golden flash—blond hair falling over the side of a face. His heart began to race, and the air around him seemed to grow heavy. He didn't need to turn fully to confirm it; he knew. It was Derrick. And he was there, behind him. Slowly, Lincoln raised his hands, almost afraid of breaking the magic of the moment. He covered Derrick's hands, which rested on his waist, and interlocked his fingers with his, bringing them together in front of his abdomen. In that instant, the noise of the night disappeared, and for the first time in his life, Lincoln felt safe, as if no one else existed— just the two of them. Lincoln crossed his fingers, wishing the world would stop, but it only paused for a fraction of a second.

"Derrick!" RedSaint's deep voice broke through like thunder. With a violent yank, he pulled Derrick away from Lincoln, breaking their contact.

Derrick, surprised, seemed to wake from a trance.Lincoln turned to them, his anxious gaze searching for Derrick, but all he found was the imposing hostility of RedSaint and Derrick wearing a wide, grotesque smile, seemingly unaware of what had just happened. There was something unsettling in his expression, in the way his eyes glinted and darted around as if searching for something, without even knowing what it was. At that moment, Lincoln didn't recognize Derrick. And in doing so, he also failed to recognize himself, questioning his blind devotion to Derrick as if the ideal he had built crumbled before his eyes.

RedSaint, noticing the confusion on Lincoln's face at Derrick's strange behavior, approached with an air of superiority. He extended his hand with a firm grip and a fake smile that felt more like a challenge than a courtesy.

"Hi, I'm RedSaint. This is my friend Derrick," he said, as if introducing a stranger and not the man who had turned Lincoln's world upside down. As he spoke, RedSaint held onto Derrick, who urgently needed to hydrate and sit down. His body seemed to be fighting off a mild overdose of ketamine and GBL, leaving him in a state of shaky alertness, as if trying not to succumb to chemical exhaustion.

"Lincoln," he replied into RedSaint's ear as he shook his hand.

Derrick, having caught the name, pulled away from RedSaint's support and, with a movement that seemed driven by a spark of recognition, grabbed Lincoln by the cheeks.

"What's your name?" he asked, looking into his eyes with interest, though his gaze bore the weight of intoxication.

"He just said it. His name is Lincoln," RedSaint interrupted, a hint of jealousy in his tone.

Derrick smiled, his eyes slightly squinting as if trying to process the information while battling the effects of the substances.

"I'm Derrick," he said with a mix of charm and disorientation. "Nice to meet you."

Lincoln didn't know how to react. The humiliation of not being recognized hit him like a cold wave, erasing any trace of the security he had felt minutes earlier. In that moment, he didn't think about his physical transformation; he only felt the sharp pain of indifference.

RedSaint, noticing the disappointment on Lincoln's face, finally acknowledged him. With a mix of anger and jealousy, he grabbed Derrick's arm and yanked him away from Lincoln. As he did, he turned to Lincoln, fixing him with a contemptuous glare, and spat in a cutting voice:

"Stay away, you freak!"

The words hit Lincoln like a dart, leaving him frozen in place. He watched helplessly as RedSaint dragged Derrick away from him. Lincoln's heart sank as he saw Derrick seemingly disappear into the shadows of the crowd. But Derrick, in a quick and determined movement, broke free from RedSaint's grip. With a furtive glance at Lincoln, he returned to him, grabbed him by the wrist, and without saying a word, led him out of the crowd with determination. RedSaint stood motionless, watching as Derrick and Lincoln vanished into the sea of men, his frustration palpable in every crack of his face. Derrick left the nightclub holding Lincoln's hand like a boyfriend, who was still sober and visibly shy. A part of the young boy wanted to hug and kiss Derrick, but his timidity held him back; though in reality, there was no need, because Derrick was already being affectionate, euphoric, and friendly. He hailed a taxi, and once seated, Lincoln noticed Derrick's hyperactivity. His feet and hands were constantly moving, and his face and chest were drenched in sweat. Lincoln, for his part, wiped the sweat away with his bare hands while discreetly observing the fine texture of his skin. Despite his inexperience, he recognized Derrick's intoxicated state, so he held his hand as if they were lovers and took note of the gold jewelry consisting of bracelets and 18-karat rings. Derrick's hand was three times more robust than Lincoln's, and just having his small hand within Derrick's, he felt like he needed nothing more.

If God willed it, he'd be fine if he died at that moment.

"Is that man in red your boyfriend?" Lincoln asked as Derrick leaned his head against the seatback, trying to calm the effects of the molly, ecstasy, GBL, and *ketamine.*

"I don't have a boyfriend, and I'm not interested."

"He's in love with you."

"And so are you," Derrick stated confidently.

"And that doesn't mean anything."

"I'm not in love with you."

"Why do people fall in love with me?" Derrick asked, staring at Lincoln, expecting an answer.

"They fall in love because..." Lincoln moved closer, touching Derrick's face as he gazed at him. "Look at yourself." Derrick smiled and looked away as if he'd heard that line a million times and had looked in the mirror just as often.

"You're all mediocre," Derrick said with a tone of contempt. Lincoln froze, having never anticipated those words.

"Stop the car, the young man has arrived," Derrick ordered the driver.

"I haven't arrived," Lincoln, uncomfortable and confused, looked out the window to see where they were: *Times Square,* then looked back at Derrick for an explanation.

"You're an idiot," Derrick said angrily, looking him in the eyes as he pushed him out of the car.

"An idiot for what?" Lincoln clung to the open door, preventing the car from leaving.

"Because I don't know what you're doing here."

"I want to get to know you."

"I'm trying to spare you the suffering."

"Why do you care?"

"What?" Derrick was confused.

"Break me," Lincoln challenged him.

"What the hell are you talking about?"

"Break me, do whatever you want, I don't care."

"You really are an idiot."

"Yes, I'm an idiot," Lincoln said, humbled and without pride. Derrick grabbed his chin to kiss him. For a moment, Derrick pretended, and his gaze softened.

"That's the problem, I don't like idiots," Derrick said, slamming the door shut, locking it, and the car drove off, leaving Lincoln helpless and heartbroken, on the verge of tears.

The car hadn't gone a block when Lincoln noticed it stopped. The rear door opened, and Derrick stuck his head out, vomiting. Lincoln smiled, and hopeful, he ran toward him.

Derrick got out of the car and ran to a trash can on the sidewalk, where he continued vomiting as the car drove away. When he finished, Lincoln offered him a bottle of water he had bought at the deli across from the trash can. Derrick glanced at him, took the bottle, and drank it down to the last drop.

Neither of them said a word. Only a satisfied smile from Lincoln sealed the moment.

When Lincoln arrived at Sofía's house, he used the keys he found in Derrick's fanny pack to enter. Adrenaline and his recent gym training allowed him to drag Derrick to the bathroom. There, with an effort fueled by determination, he placed Derrick in the bathtub and removed his clothes. Without thinking too much, he also stripped himself, letting the warm shower water cascade over them both.

Derrick woke up disoriented, his heavy eyelids barely lifting as he struggled to focus on Lincoln's face. Confusion was written across his expression as his drug-clouded mind tried to make sense of the situation.

"What are you doing?" Derrick asked, his voice hoarse, barely a whisper.

Lincoln looked at him and smiled, a mix of pride and tenderness on his face, as if taking care of Derrick was a heroic act.

"Taking care of you," he replied, smug yet gentle.

Derrick frowned and rolled his eyes, exhausted, as he tried to stand. The warm water fell over his skin, but he didn't seem to fully register it. He stumbled out of the shower, wobbling toward the sink, where he gripped it with both hands, breathing heavily.

"Where's RedSaint?" he asked suddenly, his voice tinged with confusion, reflecting the mental fog the drugs had left behind.

Lincoln froze, startled by the question. His lips parted slightly, but he couldn't immediately find an answer.

"I don't know..." he said softly. "You're with me now."

"Get dressed and get out of here," Derrick growled, staring at his reflection in the mirror, avoiding any eye contact with Lincoln.

Disappointed and pensive, Lincoln stayed under the shower water, feeling the warm droplets trying to soothe the tumult of emotions swirling inside him. As he tried to think of a way to stay, a sound from the room caught his attention.

It was Derrick, seemingly wiping his nose but, in reality, snorting ketamine with precise, almost mechanical movements.

Suddenly, Derrick reappeared at the bathroom door, wrapped in a towel. His hair was still dripping, and his eyes gleamed with a strange intensity. Without saying a word, he extended a hand toward Lincoln, revealing a small white pill—Euphorix—in his palm.

Lincoln stared at him, confused for a moment, but before he could ask anything, his desire not to break the fragile moment between them took over. He took the pill and swallowed it immediately, without hesitation or question.

Derrick offered a faint, mysterious smile and walked toward the sink. From his phone, he activated the speakers, filling the room with techno music. At the same time, the lighting changed; red lights began to pulse in rhythm with the music, transforming the space into a surreal, almost hypnotic environment.

Lincoln turned off the shower, wrapped himself in a white towel, and observed with precision the shift in Derrick's personality from a safe distance. Then, he began to feel something different in his body. His breathing quickened, his skin started to glisten with unexpected sweat, and his feet, at first without him noticing, began tapping incessantly against the bathroom floor. His fingers also began searching for something, as if trying to grasp onto something tangible amidst his altered state.

The red lights in the bathroom intensified the glow in his now-narrowed eyes, as Lincoln, struggling against the confusion, tried to keep himself steady.

Derrick, watching him out of the corner of his eye while applying his skincare products, let out a light, almost mocking laugh.

"Come here," Derrick ordered, his tone calm but with a hint of authority.

Lincoln, with erratic movements, approached and let himself be guided. Derrick easily lifted him by the waist, sitting him on the sink counter. As he applied skincare products to Lincoln's face with delicate movements, Lincoln watched him, mesmerized, as if the world had reduced itself to just the two of them and the pulsating space of the bathroom.

"We're going to have such beautiful children together," Lincoln murmured suddenly, his voice dragged by the intoxication.

Derrick paused for a moment, surprised by the statement. For the first time that night, he let out a brief, dry laugh that felt more like a reflex than a response.

Encouraged by the laugh, Lincoln brought his hands to Derrick's face, touching him gently as his eyes sought a deeper connection.

"Look at you..." Lincoln said, as if that explained everything.

Derrick looked at him with a mix of weariness and skepticism but didn't respond. Instead, he let the music fill the silence between them, creating an almost palpable tension.

Both were trapped in a moment that was both beautiful and destructive, as if the bathroom had transformed into a stage where their lives collided with equal parts force and fragility.

Later, Derrick and Lincoln sat on the edge of the bed, with a crystal bong resting on Lincoln's lap. Derrick lit the lighter and patiently heated the spherical cavity where he had placed small particles of *crystal meth*. As it heated, the particles turned into a dense cloud of smoke in the tube of the device, ready to be inhaled. When the cloud of smoke was prepared, Derrick brought the mouthpiece of the bong to Lincoln's lips. Obediently, Lincoln inhaled the smoke and then exhaled, but Derrick noticed that he hadn't inhaled properly. Acting as a mentor, he taught him the correct technique. That night, Lincoln didn't know that what he had smoked was crystal meth. In fact, he had no idea what it was and had never heard of the drug before, much less its effects. However, unknowingly, he had already witnessed its consequences, having judged many homeless people without understanding their situation.

"Is this your mother?" Lincoln asked as he picked up the framed photo on the nightstand. In the photo, a young Derrick stood with a guitar, next to a woman with dark hair and a slender figure. Derrick didn't answer; he just gazed at the photo with a mix of nostalgia and anger.

"Where is she?" Lincoln asked, intrigued.

"In Connecticut," Derrick replied, not taking his eyes off the photo of his mother.

"Do you play the guitar, do you sing?" Lincoln asked.

Derrick shrugged modestly. There was an unsettling light in his eyes.

"Sing me something, anything," Lincoln implored.

Derrick looked at him, but something in his eyes darkened drastically. Lincoln sensed the change, unaware that methamphetamine manifests as a mood disorder.

Without breaking his inquisitive gaze, Derrick pushed Lincoln onto the bed, pounced on him, and began licking his mouth and face like a dog.

For the next four hours, Lincoln and Derrick surrendered to a wild, chaotic passion, their bodies speaking a language of undeniable chemistry. Lincoln seemed to give himself over completely, yet his teeth sank into the pillow, his fingers gripping the sheets as if anchoring himself. Derrick, savage and fueled by the drugs, dominated him with a ferocity that bordered on destruction, each moment breaking Lincoln apart while binding him closer.

Beneath Derrick's ferocity lay the ghost of his past, shaping every action. When he was eight, his mother abandoned him, and his grandfather-his only source of stability-died soon after. The loss left him to face a childhood defined by loneliness and pain. By fourteen, desperation and curiosity led him into the arms of a predatory neighbor, marking his first sexual experience. From that moment, Derrick learned a cruel truth: he could redirect his inner torment outward, finding release in harming others instead of himself.

The rain pattered softly against the window, its steady rhythm cutting through the harsh sounds that filled the room. Lincoln, caught beneath the weight of Derrick sweating on top of him and his growing unease, turned toward the sound. The subtle tapping of the rain heightened his discomfort, confirming suspicions he couldn't quite articulate.

"It's raining... it's raining," he murmured, glancing at the closed window and reaching out towards the curtain. However, some arms are shorter than the desire.

"Don't move! If you move, I'd hurt you," said Derrick, impatient, eager to finish his purpose.

With effort, he slipped out from under Derrick's oppressive weight, ran to the window, pulled back the curtains, and saw the torrential rain falling outside.

Lincoln faked a smile as if he had never seen the rain before. He covered himself in white sheets and ran barefoot into the street. In the middle of the deserted avenue, as the water drenched him, he knelt and cried like a baby, releasing the carnal and emotional pain of being silently *abused*.

"Hey, get back here right now!" Derrick shouted, annoyed and dazed, standing in the doorway, dressed only in a gray sweatpants.

"Come back here right now, or the octopus will get you," he ordered.

Lincoln heard the word "*octopus*," but he didn't understand what Derrick meant. "Come on, the water feels great," he responded, calling out to him.

Derrick, under the shelter of the roof, continued gesturing for him to come back inside, but Lincoln didn't want to return to him, to that bed; he just wanted to be out, in the rain. To attract Derrick's attention, he began to dance, provoking Derrick's anger as he refused to obey.

Forced, Derrick ran towards him, grabbed him by the arm, and pulled him back into the house, repeating over and over, "The octopus is going to get you."

In her pajamas, Sofía Passeri approached the front door just as Derrick locked it and leaned against it, panting.

"Derrick, what's going on, and why are you here again?" she asked angrily, looking at Lincoln.

"Lock yourself in your room, Sofía," Derrick ordered.

"The octopus again?" she asked, suspecting the answer.

"Go to sleep, it won't get in here," Derrick assured.

"You, get out of here before I call the police!" Sofía snapped at Lincoln.

Lincoln, with no debt to anyone, trembled with nerves when she mentioned the police.

"He can't leave through here," Derrick said to Lincoln, pointing at the door while quickly analyzing all the exits in the house. "He can't leave through any of them," he concluded, looking seriously at Sofía and then at Lincoln.

"Derrick, I don't want *meth-heads* in my house," Sofía said angrily.

Lincoln, drenched from the rain, stood between Sofía and Derrick, trying to understand what they were talking about. Despite Derrick's strange behavior, he assumed the octopus was an enemy of Derrick who could arrive at any moment. Like Derrick, he also watched the door.

Angry and with her patience exhausted, Sofía appeared with Lincoln's clothes and his cell phone. She threw them at him and pushed him toward the door. "Get out of here!"

"Sofía, don't open the door!" Derrick warned.

"Son, lock yourself in your room right now," Sofía ordered, while Derrick, fearing the door, backed away with trepidation.

"Ma'am, why are you kicking me out? I didn't do anything."

"Don't come back here and leave my grandson alone. Do you wanna kill him with that *tina* trash?

"*Tina?*" Lincoln asked, confused. "Who the hell is Tina?"

Sofía slammed the door in his face.

"Ma'am, I don't know who *Tina* is," Lincoln explained desperately, banging on the door. "Ma'am, who is *Tina?*"

Disappointed and confused, Lincoln gave up and looked through the window, watching Sofía argue with Derrick. Noticing his unsettling presence on the street, Sofía ran to the window and closed the curtains.

The walk in the rain to Hell's Kitchen was not just a journey but a constant battle against his own thoughts, which seemed to multiply with every step. That night, Lincoln couldn't sleep, believing that his *insomnia* could only mean one thing: he was falling deeply in love with Derrick. What he didn't know was that he was experiencing the complex side effects of *methamphetamine* for the first time.

———

The next day, Lincoln didn't wake up, because he never slept. Despite the fever and a cold piercing his chest, anxiety drove him to put on Derrick's black hoodie, his only comfort. With the hood covering his face, he took the train to Sofía's house, propelled by an uncontrollable need to see him. Upon arriving, he knocked insistently, pounding with such force that his knuckles turned red. He waited, his eyes fixed on the windows, searching for any sign of life. From inside, Sofía heard the knocking clearly but chose to ignore it. To her, Lincoln was an unnecessary burden, and her grandson already had too many. Derrick, on the other hand, didn't hear a thing. In his room, he lay fast asleep, his breathing steady and his muscles relaxed, thanks to a dose of Xanax Sofía had diluted into his water under the pretense of vitamins. This method, perfected years ago with her daughter when drugs had turned their home into a battlefield, was now her desperate solution. She had no qualms about using the same trick with her grandson, ensuring them both a small measure of peace.

Lincoln stayed outside for two long hours. Every time he thought about leaving, hope held him back. Maybe the next minute would be the moment the door opened, or Derrick would appear around the corner, with that indecipherable smile that made him forget everything. But the minutes piled up like the clouds darkening the sky, and reality hit with the same force as the cold April wind.Finally, defeated, he turned away. The hood of Derrick's black hoodie hid his face, but his hunched shoulders betrayed his despair. Under the drizzle beginning to fall, the rejection that accompanied him started to harden, transforming into a fury he didn't know how to contain.That same night, unable to stay still in his room, he ended up at the gym. There was no plan, just an urgent need to move, to expel the chaos consuming him. In the corner of the room, a punching bag hung silently, unmoving. Something about its stillness provoked him. Lincoln approached, his heavy steps echoing in the empty space.He clenched his fists, and without fully knowing what he was doing, struck the bag. The first impact hurt his knuckles, but he didn't stop. His disordered punches began to resonate, his muscles burning with every movement. With each hit, words formed in his mind—first as murmurs, then as clearer phrases, each soaked in his frustration and pain.

"Damn the octopus..." he muttered through gritted teeth, striking harder. The words flowed, matching the rhythm of his punches, his breathing growing ragged. He didn't know where they came from, but he clung to them as if they were an anchor in the middle of his internal storm.

"Damn the octopus that has already been cursed a thousand times..."

The punches continued, and his thoughts turned into verses, each one opening new cracks in his heart. Finally, exhausted, he rested his sweaty forehead against the bag, letting the tears flow freely. In that moment, the poem was his. It was all he had.

The next morning, he recited it to the class.

Cursed be the octopus that
has already been cursed a
thousand times.

If I found you crawling on
land, with my own hands I'd
return you to the depths of the
ocean.

Cursed be the octopus that
has already been cursed a
thousand times.

If I found you in the depth of
the ocean, I'd make you a prisoner
of my dreams and tear you apart
in my nightmares.

Cursed be the octopus that
has already been cursed a
thousand times.

If in my nightmares I found
you broken and destroyed, I'd hide
you beneath the rocks.

Because if he finds out I
didn't leave you alive,
    With his bare hands, he'd kill
me dead.

Cursed be the octopus that I
myself have cursed a thousand
times.

```
Let me find you, cursed
octopus, who has already been
cursed a thousand times.
```

Linda found the prose entertaining and filled with vivid imagery, but it was his attachment to his writing that concerned her the most. As a writer, she knew that Lincoln's late work was coming from painful places full of sorrow and distress, but she preferred not to know, only to read, and experience. After class, Linda approached Lincoln, looked him in the eyes, and analyzed him. Unlike other times when he was always anxious and begging for a chance to be her assistant, this time he seemed distant and preoccupied with his own personal matters that had nothing to do with her or what she can do for him.

"Next Monday, be at my office at *The New Yorker* at 1 p.m.," she said, not very convinced. Sudden happiness filled Lincoln's body in small waves, slowly processing what was happening.

"If you are one minute late, don't bother coming, and don't return to my class. Is that clear?"

"Are you serious?" he asked, doubtful, while his heart seemed ready to leap out of his chest. Linda didn't respond because, by that moment, she had already regretted her decision. She started to leave the room when suddenly she heard Lincoln shouting at the top of his lungs as his heart seemed to explode with joy.

If Linda gave him the opportunity to be her assistant, he would no longer have to work on the streets convincing kids of his fake superpowers, and he would have all the time to show the world what a great writer he was—or at least, so he believed.

———

At midnight on Friday, without any prior appointment, Lincoln waited for Derrick at the entrance of the nightclub, fully hoping to see him. But with the long wait came existential confusion stemming from the unanswered question of why more than forty text messages he had sent to Derrick in a matter of minutes appeared in green text bubbles instead of blue. With few options, he decided to do what he did best: stay optimistic and keep waiting while continuing to send messages. It wasn't just the waiting he was trying to endure, but also his eagerness to read him a poem that couldn't wait any longer. And for those who wait, elsewhere someone else is waiting for them, so Lincoln received a call from Santiago, interrupting the unexpected wait with a proposal that would change the course of his night and the unfortunate wait.

Lincoln walked five and a half blocks from the nightclub to a five-star hotel adorned with fake gold. By the elevator stood Santiago in hotel slippers, who unusually hugged him and whispered in his ear, thanking him for coming so promptly. Lincoln quickly forgot about Derrick, as he found himself immersed in Santiago's suspicious behavior, whose gaze was more intense than a new lightbulb.

"Have you ever been with a man?" Santiago asked fearlessly, leaving Lincoln in shock.

"No!" Lincoln replied without thinking, observing how the embarrassment rose between them, waiting to see who would break first. "And you?" he asked, trying to decide if Santiago was high or drunk.

"No!" Santiago responded with aversion. "But I would with you, if it was for money."

Lincoln looked at him, surprised, and his gaze offended Santiago.

"Shut up!" Santiago pushed him lightly, with a nervous laugh that betrayed him instead of protecting him. But Lincoln knew little about body language.

"How much?" Lincoln asked with the same curiosity that killed the cat.

They both took the elevator, and Santiago guided him to a room whose nightly rate on a weekday didn't go below $2000. Inside, there would be a man nearing his 50s, married with children, sitting in an armchair facing the bed. His real name hadn't been shared, but he called himself *Discreto*. The only reason he was there was that he meticulously and repeatedly created conflicts at home to have an excuse to sleep elsewhere and hire escorts, as his pleasure consisted of watching them make love for hours. Under no circumstances did he touch them or let them touch him, not even a handshake in greeting. He also entertained no conversation with them, as he considered it beneath his intelligence.

In the bathroom, Santiago and Lincoln locked themselves in. On the marble countertop, Santiago had an array of drugs on display: euphorix, ecstasy, cocaine, ketamine, and GBL. Most of them Lincoln recognized from Derrick's cabinet, but he was curious not to see the crystal pipe.

"You haven't done drugs, have you?" Santiago asked, almost convinced the answer would be no.

"No!" Lincoln replied. "Never," he added sarcastically, but Santiago didn't notice.

"Drugs are very tricky. They're like alcohol, but without all the calories."

"I didn't know you used drugs, nor that you were a prostitute."

"I'm not a prostitute! He's a friend, and what we're doing is a favor, and the money is just a way to show his appreciation, understand?" he asked, looking him in the eyes to make him believe it. But Lincoln's innocence began to corrupt because he didn't believe him. So he turned his attention to the display of drugs on the marble countertop.

"Have you seen those crystals that you cook in a pipe, like marijuana but they're crystals?" he asked, not knowing the danger of the question.

"Methamphetamine?" Santiago asked angrily. "You smoked that shit?"

"No!" he lied, because the tone of his voice and the dilation of his pupils revealed that whatever those crystals were, they were forbidden. "That shit will drive you crazy. If I see you smoking that shit, I'll rip your head off, got it?" Lincoln nodded, and of course he understood, so much so that for the first time in almost half an hour, he thought about Derrick and the octopus. Lincoln kept his secret, and both consumed half a pill of euphorix and a dose of GBL.

Santiago taught Lincoln how to clean out, which, in other words, meant douching. Lincoln had no idea about douching: the practice of removing feces to prepare for anal penetration. There are dozens of ways to execute the task, from using a bottle of water to inserting fingers for extraction, or even using a hose. Santiago handed Lincoln an enema filled with water and instructed him to insert it into his rectum, squeeze the balloon, hold the water for about five minutes, and then evacuate. Disgusted, Lincoln initially refused to try, but the options were limited, and the need was urgent.

When Lincoln asked Santiago to leave the bathroom so he could douche in private, Santiago refused, insisting he needed to stay to give the lesson. Reluctantly, Lincoln cleaned out in front of him, continuing until the water coming out was crystal clear.

In just two hours, Santiago and Lincoln made love and received $ 5K in donations—prostitutes often refer to payment as a "donation," since no Christian has ever been jailed for donating, but many have been for paying for sex services. From the $5K donated to a "good cause," Lincoln earned $3K simply for being a supposed virgin, which he was not. After concluding the performance for the conflicted man, who stayed in the hotel searching on the internet for another duo, Santiago decided to take Lincoln to a straight nightclub. The experience in bed had forged a natural physical closeness between them, heightened by the intoxication, leading to them touching each other more frequently than usual. The subtle sense of brotherhood took an unexpected turn when Natalie caught Santiago emerging from the bathroom, pushing Lincoln against the wall. "Santiago," she called out. Santiago turned and kissed her passionately, leaving Lincoln in stunned silence against the wall.

"Aren't you going to introduce me to your friend?" Natalia asked Santiago while studying Lincoln.

Santiago played dumb, as he always did when he found himself in an uncomfortable and reserved position. Without much fuss, Natalia rolled her eyes and introduced herself as Santiago's girlfriend. Lincoln nearly had a heart attack, but no one noticed, not even the woman standing in front of him. Recognizing the state of ecstasy of the two men, Natalia offered free drinks, boasting that she knew the owners of the nightclub.

"And what do you own?" Lincoln asked, with the mere intention of putting her down.

76

Natalia was stunned. Lincoln's cruel intention was received with satisfaction.

"I'm still studying," she retorted, undeterred.

"Then you should introduce us to your friend," he said with an arrogance that had cost him $ 3000, paid for with the sweat of his *ass*. As much as Santiago tried to play dumb, he heard Lincoln's rudeness. So, with a sudden jerk, he dragged him to the bathroom. Santiago had a reputation to uphold, and Lincoln's attitude was becoming a liability.

"What's wrong with you?" Santiago asked angrily.

Lincoln exploded, feeling offended, especially after what had happened between them in that hotel room.

"Your girlfriend? What the hell?"

"Is there a problem?"

"What do you mean you have a girlfriend?" Lincoln was resentful. "I still have your cum inside me."

Santiago shoved him to shut him up. "Shut up! What's wrong with you?" Santiago muttered, looking around to see who might have heard. With rage, he cornered him and clarified through gritted teeth, "I'm not a faggot."

In a moment of tension, Lincoln froze, mid-reply, catching sight of Derrick exiting the bathroom. His heart raced, determined to reach him, he spat in Santiago's face: "No, you're not a faggot; you just let yourself get fucked for money," then shoved him aside with a swift arm movement Santiago hadn't anticipated. With the urgency of Carmen Maura in *Women on the Verge of a Nervous Breakdown*, Lincoln rushed after Derrick, leaving Santiago fuming with anger. Enraged, Santiago chased after him, but Lincoln flipped him off and disappeared into the crowd, hoping to find the missing Derrick.

All night, Lincoln couldn't find Derrick, and the text messages he sent received no reply. Arriving home alone with the effects of the drugs splitting his head, he doubted whether he had really seen Derrick or if it had been a beautiful optical illusion he wished to dream about. But he couldn't sleep, nor did he eat a bite. To pass the time, he masturbated for hours watching pornography on the internet until the drugs wore off, and then he fell into a deep sleep.

———

By midday Monday, Lincoln was already up. He dressed in a *ridiculous* military green floral shirt, slicked back his hair, and gathered his collection of most cherished writings. With the hope of getting a job as Linda's assistant, he ventured out to the streets, heading to *The New Yorker* offices, burdened by negative thoughts questioning the true reason for his existence. What the poor soul didn't know was that these thoughts and the overwhelming fatigue were another side effects of the drugs: *lack of purpose*.

Upon reaching the traffic light at 54th Street and 9th Avenue, he noticed something that would change the course of his day. Ignoring the red light, he crossed the street without looking, angering a few drivers as he made his way toward Derrick Passeri, who was sitting at a table behind the restaurant's window. The sight of Derrick had set something wild loose inside him—no words would satisfy; he wanted answers, he wanted rage, he wanted *blood*.

The waitress taking Derrick and RedSaint's order noticed the suspicious young man in a floral shirt with an angry face, reminding her of one of her ex-boyfriends—not all of them, just the ones who had hit her. Then the bang-bang of Lincoln's fist against the window startled her, and without taking the order, she left. RedSaint rolled his eyes upon seeing Lincoln, while Derrick remained hidden behind his dark sunglasses. He was too tired to intervene, their party weekend was still not over. When Lincoln arrived at the table, RedSaint said with the seriousness of a machine gun, "That's the fucking problem with eating their ass so well."

Derrick didn't flinch; he had had a weekend full of sex, drugs, and other addictions that left him with no energy to entertain a lovesick teenager who barely knew how to clean himself.

"Why haven't you answered my messages?" Lincoln asked, introducing his aggressive arrival at the table.

No response.

"If he's ignoring you, he's not interested," RedSaint laughed. "Any other stupid questions, or are you leaving so we can finish here?"

"Who asked for your opinion?" Lincoln retorted, spitting the words at him, his courage perhaps determined by his visible anger or the residue of drugs in his system that still gave him an air of grandeur.

"I would gladly smash that big head of yours, but it took us 45 minutes to get this table and the entire damn night to eat these pancakes. So today, unlike any other day, I'm going to allow you to leave on your own, with your dignity intact. And the next time you see me, you won't look at me and you'll turn around like a dog, or else I'll smash your head against the ground even if I'm starving." The gravity of his words hung in the air, emphasizing the severity of the consequences.

"I'm not leaving." His voice trembled, but he kept his gaze steady. "Make me."

RedSaint grabbed him by the neck and it didn't take much effort to drag him through the restaurant and throw him out onto the street like something used, dirty and old.

———

The Dean's Dungeon was a two-bedroom apartment with a basement in the heart of Hell's Kitchen, where Sam and Dean once lived happily. Dean, a flight attendant, and Sam, his partner, initially planned to spend New Year's apart due to their respective commitments. They agreed to reunite on *Atlantis*—a gay cruise—after the holidays. However, their plans took a turn when Dean decided to return to New York City to surprise Sam. But the surprise led to a heated confrontation when Dean found Sam having a sex party in their transformed, neon-lit apartment. Following a lengthy quarrel, the guests left, and Dean, feeling frustrated, called off their relationship. This decision had a cascading effect on Dean's life; he lost his job and fell into the trap of depression that he succumbed to with sex and drugs, and when financial issues arose, Dean saw his neon-lit apartment as an opportunity to make money.

Derrick and RedSaint walked from the restaurant to *The Dean's Dungeon*. Before leaving the restaurant, where only RedSaint ate, they both went to the bathroom and consumed molly and *ketamine*. By the time they arrived at Dean's Dungeon, they were no longer the same.

Lincoln arrived 30 seconds later at Dean's building, with scratches on his hands and forearms from the fall. The front door was locked, so using an old New York tactic, he persistently rang all the buzzers until someone finally let him in. Two men, aged between 40 and 45, were exiting the apartment at the end of the hallway, dressed in athletic wear with leather accessories, emanating a very carnal sexual vibe and a look that evoked either fear or intrigue. By then, Lincoln had become somewhat less naive, beginning to develop a cunning nature. Following his instinct, he ventured into the apartment at the end of the hallway, where he found a vibrant interior, illuminated with neon lights and techno music that spread through the space like a curtain of smoke. Behind a drywall partition, in front of an old computer, sat a trans woman with a bare torso. She denied Lincoln entry for his audacity in presenting a fake ID. Lincoln tried to persuade her, but she, nearly twenty years his senior, asked him to leave. However, his persistence guaranteed him entry at the exorbitant cost of $200.

The place was so small that even a modest crowd on the street seemed like a large congregation inside. Lincoln appeared from behind the curtains, nervous from the sexual energy emanating from the place. He leaned against the wall in his *Calvin Klein* briefs, which looked like an old coffee strainer. He searched for Derrick among the crowd but found no familiar faces. Overwhelmed, he sought refuge in the bathroom, where he encountered a man around 65 years old, so frail that a gust of wind could blow him away. The man was inspecting a small bag of white powder that Lincoln instantly recognized but couldn't discern whether it was cocaine or *ketamine*. The man recognized the craving in Lincoln's eyes and, without preamble, offered him *ketamine*. Lincoln approached, took the bag, and prepared a generous line of white powder on a key. He inhaled so deeply that he felt the effect rise to his temples.

From the bathroom door, RedSaint watched Lincoln inhaling through the second nostril while the frail man was already on his knees in front of Lincoln's worn-out briefs.

"What are you doing?" Lincoln asked the 65-year-old man arrogantly, noticing RedSaint's presence at the door.

"You said..." the man began, confused.

"Who are you?" Lincoln interrupted with a pedantic attitude, elevating his spirits to the same height as the ketamine. "Are you stalking me?" he added.

Intimidated, the 65-year-old man stood up and left, avoiding being expelled from the only place where he still felt alive.

Feeling proud of his act of treating someone like the dirt on a shoe he couldn't afford, Lincoln projected his masculine energy around RedSaint. RedSaint approached the sink and spat, disgusted by what he had witnessed. By then, the ketamine's effect manifested in waves that left Lincoln's vision blurry for a few seconds, forcing him to crouch for stability. Without intervening, RedSaint watched him without any sign of concern. When the effect became manageable, Lincoln looked up at him, and RedSaint extended his hand. Lincoln didn't hesitate to take his hand, because no matter how much he hated him, he would always admire him for everything he was and that Lincoln would never be in his entire life. Holding RedSaint's hand, Lincoln descended a staircase leading to a basement, a small and dark room where a sling barely fit. Upon entering and seeing the "EXIT" sign at the top of the wall, Lincoln experienced a strange sense of *déjà vu*, which he ignored because he was already aroused and began to display his social skills, exuding uninhibited humor due to the effects of the *ketamine* and the intense sexual scene before him: a man in a sling being used by five men. Lincoln counted them with his index finger twice to make sure he wasn't mistaken. The men laughed at Lincoln's silly comments. When someone asked what he was doing there, he replied that he was looking for his boyfriend, asking if anyone had seen him. Laughter spread.

It was too dark to see their faces, but Derrick watched him silently from the sling while a man was taking care of him.

"Maybe," RedSaint answered his question with a satisfied tone.

Lincoln looked at him, and despite being intoxicated, knew Derrick was there, so he began to closely examine the ugly faces of those men, making the moment funny for them but dark for him. Approaching the figure controlling Derrick, he discovered a slim man of medium height, with thick lips, skin color indeterminate in the darkness, and an intimidating face, the only one not laughing. Lincoln turned his gaze to the man hanging in the sling, fearing what he might find. And in the shadows, he recognized Derrick watching him, examining him with a fake smile as if Lincoln's life was breaking in two. Without thinking, Lincoln slapped him, leaving his hand red and Derrick's cheek burning. RedSaint kept his promise, grabbing Lincoln's head and smashing it against the wall with such force that it left him unconscious immediately.

When he woke up, the first face he saw was that of the trans woman at the entrance, to whom he had paid $200 for access. She was the one who expelled him from *The Dean's Dungeon.*

———

Susan Loft was 48 years old, and in any ordinary mirror, she'd appear over 50. But in her own mirror, she managed to look barely 40, and since the forties are the new thirties, she would dress in form-fitting attire, showcasing her legs and décolletage. In the bygone era when she was considered a knockout, her breasts had possessed a captivating beauty, but over time, the grasping hands of many men had gradually chipped away at their allure, leaving them now as a simple functional assets.

When Susan Loft returned home, her street was swarmed by police, media, and ambulances in response to a recent mass shooting. If it hadn't been for Susan's obsession with winning the lottery, she wouldn't have found herself waiting 15 minutes for the deli's cashier to arrive, and if she hadn't waited those 15 minutes, she would have been shot in the forehead and saved a couple of dollars on a losing ticket.

Upon entering her building, she felt a peace leaving the chaos behind, but upon opening the door to his apartment, she found a much bigger mess. She naively thought they had been robbed, but the most valuable thing in that apartment was a six-pack of Bud Light in the fridge, and that day, it was no longer six, but two.

"Lincoln!" Susan shouted, inspecting the apartment, which was turned upside down, until she found Lincoln sitting on the floor in the corner, elbows on his knees, staring at the window through which the intermittent light of police cars shone. He was no longer crying, even though he wanted to, he couldn't, because his tear ducts had dried up like riverbeds. Susan crouched in front of him, remembering the important date he had with Linda at *The New Yorker*, and quickly assumed that the disaster in the apartment was the result of rejection.

"You don't need those people who know nothing," she said, as annoyed as she was offended. "You are Lincoln Sorni, the great writer!" Without having read a book in her life and without having read Lincoln's writings, but inspired, she raised her arms in the air, "You write, my prince, write everything that comes from here," touching his chest, "and don't believe them..."

Lincoln interrupted her speech by grabbing the hand resting on his chest with force, "I want to kill him," he confessed as his eyes filled with tears.

"Kill who?" she asked, confused, as Lincoln debated whether or not to tell her about the recent events in his life. Although she was not stupid, she was very experienced and knowledgeable about love, but even more so about heartbreak. It was impossible for her not to have knowledge in this regard, with all the times she had failed looking for love, but by that day, she understood that the problem with looking for love is finding it where it no longer exists.

"Who is this man? Because it is a man, isn't it?" she asked, curious.

Lincoln handed her his old, now cracked, iPhone, revealing a photo of Derrick as the wallpaper. Susan raised her right eyebrow in response to the surprise, but also to the confusion of seeing a man like Lincoln dating someone as handsome as Derrick.

"That's him?" she let out a short laugh, ridiculing the drama.

Lincoln did not answer, feeling belittled by her obvious implication. Susan handed him the phone and stood up, ignoring the now unnecessary drama.

"Are you not going to say anything?" he shouted, offended.

"Pick up this mess."

"I want him to suffer!" he shouted with a force that exposed his own suffering.

"I want him to suffer!" Susan mocked, imitating him. "Men like my brother Joe don't suffer. They use you and turn you into *shit*, so get up and clean up this mess, because I'm not your maid," she shouted with such force that she exposed her own suffering and her darkest secret. Then she locked herself in her bedroom and didn't come out all night, but Lincoln could hear her crying.

———

Lincoln cried during the day and slept through the night on his phone. Derrick didn't possess Lincoln's phone number, and even if he did, he wouldn't have made the call. Sadness often operates quietly, slowly morphing into anger over time. Unlike sadness, anger is a loud emotion and can lead to consequential decisions. Initially, Lincoln sought relief by venting his frustrations through punching pillows, but this gradually evolved into using a punching bag at the gym.

One day, at around 5:45 pm, a Christian had been waiting patiently for the punching bag for quite some time. Lincoln had been using it for an hour, but his punches lacked technique, and he ended up hurting his knuckles, infuriating the patient Christian, who knew better how to punch a bag. "How long, bro?" he asked politely, but Lincoln responded harshly, "Fuck off!" If Lincoln had known about the Christian's true character, he might have responded differently.

The Christian was a good person on a daily basis but with an obscure past of violent incidents. A jury in the state of New York ordered him to undergo therapy for the rest of his life. If Lincoln hadn't been so furious, he might have landed in the clinic with facial fractures. Nonetheless, the confrontation was a fair one, resulting in both men having the other's blood on their hands. That was the first and last time that those two men saw each other, and that was the last time that Lincoln set foot in that gym. The Christian went to therapy right after the incident, and Lincoln got on the F train towards Harlem to pay a necessary visit.

When he arrived at Sofía's house, he knocked on the door and rang the bell so many times that he felt like crying out of rage and helplessness. And when Sofía, who was walking back home with her grocery bag, saw him almost breaking the doorbell, she shouted from the street:

"If you damage the doorbell, you're paying for it," she warned.

Lincoln turned to her and, with a defiant attitude, approached.

"Where's Derrick?"

"Derrick?" Sofía asked, confused. "His name is Kenny, not Derrick."

"His name isn't Derrick?" Lincoln asked, as angry as he was confused, his face burning as if he had just been slapped.

"His name is Kenny Passeri, but his problem is that he thinks he's from a better family, and well, no, he doesn't live here either. So do me a favor and look for him somewhere else," she concluded, walking towards the house.

Lincoln had noticed since he first visited that he didn't live there, but he never asked.

"He's at his mother's house," Lincoln lied with a confidence that could equal two well-told lies. Something about his words resonated with Sofía, so without haste but with much intrigue, she turned to him.

"And if you know he's at his mother's, why don't you look for him there, at his mother's?"

"Because I lost the address," he argued. "Could you give me the address?" he asked, lowering his guard.

Sofía studied Lincoln as if he were the result of a medical exam.

"The face, did he do that to your face?" she asked, referring to the bruises.

"No!" he answered, sharply, feeling the bruises.

"And he told you where his mother lives?"

"Connecticut," Lincoln replied vehemently.

Sofía nodded, disappointed.

"I won't let him know I got it from you," implored.

Sofía never understood why Derrick lied about his mother; she thought he had overcome the trauma.

"His mother is in the cemetery, two blocks down," she confessed. "I wish you the best of luck."

She never understood where her grandson inherited this need for lying from. It had to be from his dead mother because, from her, it could be possible. Sofía only lied to her followers on YouTube; otherwise, she lived a very honorable life, or at least that's what she thought.

"That's a lie," he expressed painfully. "He told me his mother lived in Connecticut."

"His mother abandoned him before he turned eight," Sofía added to her story with a certain detachment. By then, she had already exorcised the demons of the past that tied her down to what was supposed to be an eternal bed of torture.

Sofía continued her way to the house, leaving Lincoln speechless in the aftermath of her confession. He couldn't find his own voice; somehow, he felt more comfortable in the silence. Then, she paused in the doorway, glancing back. "Want to hear a story?" she asked.

Lincoln nodded.

"When his mother died, Kenny disappeared," she began, her voice distant. "The whole city of New York knew about it. The police suspected a possible kidnapping. They questioned his mother's friends—criminals, addicts, for the most part, all despicable beings—but found nothing." She paused, glancing over at the old house on the corner, and Lincoln's gaze followed hers.

"Then, on the third day," she continued, "Kenny walked into the house as if nothing had happened. He sat in the old armchair and watched his cartoons on TV."

Sofía's gaze drifted to the window. "From that window," she murmured, "he watched as my world came crashing down with my daughter's death... and the agony of his disappearance."

Lincoln turned to Sofía to find her lost in the memories of those cursed days.

After his mother's abandonment, Derrick hid in the old house across the street. Its owners had a beautiful five-bedroom residence in California, and for most of the year, the New York house remained empty. He found a way to enter without breaking a single window, and in the solitude of the space, he consoled himself.

Sofía never told her grandson who his mother really was, because she didn't want her daughter's mistakes to be used against her as a grandmother. But in the end, it didn't matter because Derrick hated her no matter what she said or did. A shame clouded her past and her present, and on many nights when her mind turned cold and his skin hard, she thanked God for taking her daughter and fervently asked Him to have mercy on her soul and give her the opportunity to reincarnate in another human body, but with a better brain.

On the last day of self-imposed captivity in the house across the street from his grandmother's, Derrick promised himself to escape from her and build a life that he owed to no one; a life that was solely his.

"Now do you want an advice or you do *not*?" She asked Lincoln, determined.

Lincoln nodded, intrigued.

"Don't waste your time, and do *not* look for him, because you won't find him."

"He's *not* gonna find me, because he's not looking for me." He shot back, desperate, vulnerable, crying. She ignored him because she had seen that movie before and already knew the ending. So, she went inside the house, just to avoid being part of it. Lincoln wiped his face and gazed at the window of the old house across the street, imagining eight-year-old Derrick, looking back at him with sad but very fixed eyes.

Was Derrick an angel or a demon? Lincoln never answered that question, but that night, only God knows, he tried.

The most unsettling thing about the effect of drugs on his body was that they betrayed him, generating a series of bitter experiences that determined for him the insignificant need to continue a life that, to him, wasn't worth living. However, the curiosity about the next minute kept him next to his phone, alive, waiting for a text or a miracle from the man who had left and taken with him everything good he knew about himself. And although his life was a piece of experience that served no purpose, he returned to *Times Square* in his Spider-Man costume to make money that no longer fulfilled him.

Santiago still seemed upset about the unresolved incident with Lincoln in the nightclub bathroom that night when Lincoln had offended his girlfriend. However, some habits are stronger than anger, Lincoln and Santiago ended up in the McDonald's bathroom, counting their earnings from the day. Lincoln took longer to finish, and as Santiago was about to leave, Lincoln said with an authoritarian tone, uncharacteristic of him,

"We're going out tonight."

"I already have plans," Santiago responded.

"Cancel them," Lincoln ordered.

"I just told you, I have plans," Santiago clarified, annoyed.

"And I just told you cancel them."

"Fuck you!" Santiago said as he started walking out, but for latinos "*Fuck you*" is a funny insult.

"Are you going out with your fat girlfriend?" Lincoln asked, feeling superior, not insulted.

Santiago wanted to hit him but chose to leave instead.

"Bring her, I don't care," Lincoln shouted as Santiago walked out. Lincoln gathered his things and followed him with a newfound confidence that, although unfamiliar, was starting to suit him.

That night, Lincoln slicked back his hair and dressed all in black. He looked like a dangerous criminal but ridiculously attractive. Something in his face was beginning to fade, perhaps the innocent laugh or the downcast gaze. Around midnight, Natalia and Santiago arrived at the *Pussies&Dickys* nightclub. Natalia didn't want to go, but Santiago had an inexplicable urge to see Lincoln. Lincoln had arrived before midnight because he was annoyed being at home and consumed by the strange need to get high. *Pussies&Dickys* was not exactly a gay-friendly establishment. Lincoln, who was far from a fan of women and heterosexual nightclubs, positioned himself in the middle of the crowd with high expectations of getting a *good high*. However, the anxiety of potentially finding Derrick in some direction kept him from reaching his desired *high* state as quickly as he wanted. Natalia, on her part, reached such a high level of intoxication that despite being fully functional, she required dedicated attention, which ruined Santiago's night as he had to hold her by the waist like a rag doll. When the *euphorix* started to kick in for Lincoln, an animalistic and shameless instinct was unleashed in him. He took every opportunity to touch Santiago discreetly on unusual parts of his body like his neck, arms, and nose, all while looking him straight in the eyes without a hint of shame. At first, Santiago was confused, then he became annoyed, but Lincoln didn't care about the rejection. Finally, when Santiago's mood improved by his own drugs, smiled, intensifying the palpable tension between the two men in the midst of the pulsating beats, turning the dance floor into a stage for a complex interplay of desires and dynamics, that's when Jo Lynn appeared among the crowd and party lights, her dark eyes locking onto Lincoln's without permission. Jo Lynn Vanderbilt was a captivating woman with red hair, a slender body in a metallic dress that she didn't wear but rather smeared on, and a European accent so fake it exuded danger. She hadn't yet turned twenty-five, and her financial life was already settled. Everything about her was sensual, and she knew everything about sex. Her first sexual experience was when she was 11 years old by her own hand with the help of a cucumber. A year later, she begged her driver, Paco Episcopal, to make her a woman. Paco Episcopal, a man of faith with a wife and kids who lived off his paycheck, refused. Jo Lynn had touched herself since a young age but got bored quickly. She flirted with her sports teacher and Paco Episcopal. Though both appeared to be easy targets, Jo Lynn chose Paco Episcopal over the teacher because he was closer and mentally poorer. Whenever she made advances to Paco Episcopal, he consistently and respectfully rebuffed her. Tired of rejection, she presented Paco with an ultimatum: if he refused to comply with her desires, she would falsely accuse him of molesting her, threatening to ensure he ended up in jail for the rest of his life. Jo Lynn was 12 at the time, but she appeared to be 15, and her breasts and hips were the size of a grown woman.

By the time Jo Lynn appeared in front of Lincoln, she hadn't changed much from the Jo Lynn Paco Episcopal once knew. However, unlike in the past, she had reached adulthood, drank alcohol like it was water, consumed drugs like a pharmacy, and distributed her body like merchandise. Jo Lynn's radiant presence, exuding a captivating sophistication, awakened a strange energy in Lincoln, as he had never before felt physically attracted to a woman. Maybe it was her dark eyes that captivated him, or that broad smile with perfect teeth, or that red hair, or those robust breasts. Perhaps it was the curiosity of feeling physically attracted to a woman, or the effect of ecstasy transgressing his own reality, or maybe it was the opportunity to make Santiago jealous. Whatever it was, before he could say a word, she lunged forward and kissed him. Out of the corner of his eye, Lincoln saw Santiago watching him, annoyed, while holding his girlfriend, who was crazier than a kite without a tail. Satisfied, Lincoln began kissing Jo Lynn passionately, using all the attributes of his mouth. Despite her extensive history with men, none had touched, kissed, cornered, or licked her mouth like a dog. Without thinking, she grabbed his hand and led him to the bathroom. There, she locked the door, pushed him against the wall, kissed him until his mouth was dry, and touched him in his intimate parts. Satisfied, she pulled out a small bag with ecstasy, pills, and cocaine from between her breasts and shared a pill with him.

"I took one of those recently," Lincoln said, refusing the pill.

"Not these," Jo Lynn assured, swapping the pill for another one and putting it in his mouth.

"Are you going to ask me to be your girlfriend?" she asked seriously, influenced by the effect of the drugs.

Lincoln didn't answer, but he did feel a jolt, raising his gaze to the ceiling, announcing the imminent departure on a psychedelic trip. Of all the thoughts he could have had, Derrick Passeri was the only one that came to mind. Looking at Jo Lynn, he saw Derrick, smiled, and kissed her as Derrick would have kissed him: with lots of saliva and a wide open mouth.

———

The next morning, Lincoln was awakened by the intermittent ringing of an insistent call, in a bed with a mattress as soft as a cloud. Without

97

opening his eyes, he was already conscious when he heard a woman's voice answering the call. Turning his head, he saw a naked woman sitting on the edge of the bed, with red hair cascading down her white back. However, what impressed him the most was the sophistication of that loft, whose name he did not know, but if someone asked him, he would say it was one of those very large apartments.

Jo Lynn had been living alone since she turned seventeen. After her parents' divorce, her father, as a consolation prize, gave his ex-wife, Hartford, an old property he had acquired as part of a payment in a poker game. None of the Vanderbilts showed any interest in the old property, which had been abandoned for years, but when Hartford grew tired of living with Jo Lynn, she found the perfect opportunity to remodel it and move her there before a tragedy occurred, because without a doubt, one of them would end up killing the other. Although the mother was not affectionate with her daughter, Hartford paid close attention to the details when remodeling the old property, which was located on the fourth floor of an old building with an industrial infrastructure of high ceilings, floor-to-ceiling windows, and fine concrete walls, situated in the heart of SoHo.

"No! I'm not canceling. I'm saying I'm on my way. What part of 'I'm on my way' don't you understand?" she yelled angrily as she quickly headed to her closet, looking for something to wear.

Lincoln took his time to remember how he got there, but no matter how much he tried to dive into his memory, he couldn't recall that night, except for Jo Lynn in the bathroom, asking him to be her boyfriend. Concluding that this woman was crazier than a loon, so, he buried his face in the pillow and fell into a deep sleep, which was abruptly interrupted by Jo Lynn pulling the covers off him.

"You need to leave now."

"But where?" he asked, groggy.

"To your house. I don't know. It's not my problem, but you need to leave because I have to go out, and you can't stay here."

"I'm not going to steal anything. Where do you need to go in such a hurry?"

"I have a medical appointment. I'm already late, and I can't miss it."

"A medical appointment on a Sunday?" he asked suspiciously.

"Yes! Can you leave already, please?"

"What kind of medical appointment is that, on a Sunday, that you can't reschedule?"

"I'm going to get an abortion, okay? Satisfied? Now, can you please leave my house? Seriously, you have to go."

When Lincoln heard the word "abortion," he was instantly awake, all the accumulated fatigue from the party was gone. The only association he had with that term was from an argument with his mother, who had yelled at him, "*You would've been worth nothing if I'd aborted you!*" Lincoln was very young when that argument took place. At school, they hadn't yet taught him the meaning of "abortion," and his mother said it knowing he didn't understand. But the huge RAE dictionary that rested in his father's small library—who wasn't really his father— alongside a yellow hardcover book titled "Sex" in pink letters, deciphered the mystery for him. In the sex book, he found pencil drawings of the procedure, explaining the process step by step. From that day on, his life was never the same, and without talking about it, he began calling his mother by her first name.

"Are you pregnant?" he said but it came out more like question.

"And why do you care?"

"If you abort, you'll regret it your whole life. Did you know they behead the babies?"

"Shut up and get out of my house or I'll call security," she threatened.

"Did you know they cut off their little legs?" he continued. Fed up with Lincoln, Jo Lynn grabbed her purse, Lincoln's clothes, and took them to the door. Lincoln looked for his underwear but couldn't find it, so he covered himself with the white blankets and followed her.

"We can talk about this, please," he implored at the door, keeping his feet inside while his clothes had been thrown into the hallway.

"Leave, please," she responded.

"Let's talk, and I promise I'll leave."

"Do whatever you want," she resigned, leaving him at the door and heading towards the elevator.

Lincoln, standing in the doorway like a tree and covered with the white sheets, was flooded with anxiety that fought against time. "Marry me," he shouted, walking towards her as she was entering the elevator. He ran and wedged his foot, preventing the door from closing. "Marry me and let's raise this baby."

"Raise it? You don't even have a job."

"I do have a job," he said, humiliated.

"What job?" she asked defiantly.

"Who needs a job when you have more money than Jesus Christ himself if he were alive?"

She looked at him, angry but thoughtful. Then she pushed him out of the elevator and said, "No."

That afternoon, after Lincoln convinced her to marry him, Jo Lynn promised not to consume any more drugs or alcohol during the pregnancy, as long as he satisfied her needs as she required. This meant Lincoln had to be constantly under the influence of GBL, Viagra, and ecstasy to fulfill his part of the deal. After the initial euphoria wore off, they both developed an unusual connection due to the depression that accompanied the side effects of the drugs. But by the fourth day, when their hormones leveled out and reality began to set in, Jo Lynn, ashamed, asked him to leave and forget about the deal. Lincoln insisted firmly on honoring his part of the agreement, because even though no one asked, he was determined not to return to his filthy old room at Susan's house.

Jo Lynn's mother would have preferred to waste her night with her friends at a *Chanel* store, buying handbags, jackets, and shoes that she would never use. But just as she once had the brilliant idea of getting pregnant, she was now obliged to attend the dinner where, for the first time, her daughter would introduce her boyfriend.

Hartford meticulously groomed her daughter to marry the heir of some European fortune, or in the worst-case scenario, a Hollywood actor of Leonardo DiCaprio or Tom Hardy's caliber. To her surprise, she found herself facing Lincoln, a half-man who, despite his *Ferragamo* suit and the perfume he had bathed in, smelled borrowed and of pure puberty. Definitely, the poor taste hadn't been inherited from her but from her father, who had an eye for lost causes, except for her, of course.

At the table, there was no talk of Lincoln or with Lincoln. Hartford had more important topics to discuss, such as Jo Lynn's university, to which she showed the slightest attention, evading the great responsibility that she would one day take over her father's companies. Lincoln remained uncomfortable in the silence, observing the broken dynamic between mother and daughter. Although he might have had his own opinion, he had no point of comparison. When the elegant waiter brought the folder with the bill, Lincoln, excited, in a hurry, and very new to the experience, grabbed it, looked at the hefty amount, raised an eyebrow, then smiled at his future wife and mother-in-law. He pulled out his new GUCCI wallet from one of the pockets of his Ferragamo suit resting on the back of his chair, extracted a credit card, placed it inside the folder, and rested it in the center of the table.

"You do know that I pay that card, right?" Hartford asked with the firm intention of humiliating him, as she grabbed the folder and placed it at the edge of the table, signaling the waiter that it was ready to be picked up.

Jo Lynn wanted to ignore her mother, but the embarrassing action was typical of her personality.

"Well, as much as you pay it, no," she said, ridiculing her mother. "Mother has never worked a day in her life," she confessed to Lincoln. "Father has always been the one with the money. It's a shame he didn't come, right, Mother?" she finished, satisfied, looking at her mother, who for the first time in her life looked so angry that she could have slapped her right at the table.

In the women's restroom, Hartford entered with an anger that seemed to consume her, and Jo Lynn followed her.

"How dare you ridicule me like that?" Hartford asked Jo Lynn as she positioned herself in front of the sink. She pulled a small gold container from her *Chanel* purse, and upon opening it, revealed a white powder. Using a tiny spoon, she scooped up the cocaine and inhaled it.

"I don't understand why you care. You've ignored him all night, and the only time you noticed him was to humiliate him."

"I want you to end this... *thing*, whatever it is you have with him. If you want to do charity work, call UNICEF, but you will not bring *peasants* into our family who can't even pronounce our last name."

"And could you pronounce the last name when you met father?"

"What did you say?" Hartford asked, as angry as she was offended.

"I'm just saying, if Father did a charitable act with you, why can't I do the same?" Jo Lynn asked boldly.

Hartford slapped her, turning her face.

"I wouldn't do that again, Mother. I'm pregnant."

Hartford was shocked by the unexpected news.

"Have you lost your mind, Jo Lynn? How can you be pregnant?" she asked, even angrier. "How could you not take care of yourself? You're even more stupid than I thought. Tomorrow we'll find a doctor and that's it. That child will not see the light of day. If your father finds out, he'll kill you and him, and then he'll kill me."

"I'm going to have it, Mother."

"You will *not* have it," Hartford assured, upset.

"I said, I *will* have it."

"And why do you want to have it?" Hartford's tone turned sharp. "Is it just to prove to the universe that you're as bad a mother as I am? Is that it?" She asked, not expecting an answer.

Jo Lynn faltered for a moment, caught off guard by the jab.

"I hope not," she said, her voice tinged with disappointment.

"Well, let me give you some news," Hartford continued, her words cutting. "Whether you like it or not, you're just like me."

"I'd rather be dead than be like you," Jo Lynn snapped.

"You're right," Hartford says with a smile, amused, though she should have been offended. "You're not exactly like me. After all, I didn't get pregnant by a *gay* man."

"He's not gay," Jo Lynn responds, her voice trembling.

"He is gay, Jo Lynn. You let yourself get pregnant by a *gay* man, and you didn't even realize it."

"I've already told you he's not *gay*, and I'm going to have this baby, Mother. So you better get used to it because we're also getting married."Hartford felt a sudden pain in her heart, grabbed the sink with one hand, and clutched her chest with the other.

Jo Lynn remained unmoved.

"I raised you to marry a *man*."

"I am the man, Mother! Me!" she approached as closer as never before, intimidating her.

Hartford forced a nervous laugh as she watched her daughter leave.

"But don't come crying to me when you find him in your bed with another man," she shouted, as she composed herself and prepared another bump of cocaine. "Loser," she muttered to herself about Jo Lynn.

————

One summer day, Jo Lynn and Lincoln had just finished making love. Jo Lynn's belly was already noticeable, and Lincoln exuded an air of grandeur reflected in his body language and the fine jewelry he wore: a *Cartier* gold bracelet and three gold chains, which he never took off for any reason. That inquisitive and unsettling look had been replaced by a sublime one, constantly maintained with *ketamine*. Sitting on the edge of the bed, Lincoln meticulously prepared a line of ketamine, his movements almost ritualistic. He inhaled deeply, his eyes locked on Jo Lynn as she walked naked toward the bathroom, her swollen belly bouncing slightly with each step.

"Jo Lynn, why have you never told me about the father of your child?" Lincoln's voice was slow, almost as if he was still floating on the effects of the drug.

Jo Lynn paused in the doorway, her body language guarded. "You never asked me," she said, not turning around to face him.

"Never?" Lincoln pressed, his voice tinged with confusion.

"The father of my child is you," Jo Lynn replied, her words simple, but carrying a weight that Lincoln wasn't expecting.

Lincoln's lips parted in surprise, a smile spreading across his face as he leaned back against the bed. He felt a wave of relief, mixed with drowsiness. "What if he comes back one day?" he asked, his words slurred slightly from the drugs.

Jo Lynn's voice came from the bathroom, distant but clear. "He won't come back."

"But what if he does?" Lincoln persisted, his mind not fully processing the conversation.

"People who never left have nowhere to return to," Jo Lynn answered with finality.

Lincoln frowned. "What you're saying doesn't make sense." He rubbed his face, trying to shake off the confusion. "I'm going to order something to eat," he mumbled, turning to get his phone. "You don't know who the father of your child is," he muttered again, more to himself than to her.

"I do," Jo Lynn said, this time coming out of the bathroom, wrapped in a towel.

"No, you don't. You don't know who the 'biological father' is," Lincoln corrected, half-opening his eyes as he stared at her, studying her reaction.

Jo Lynn ignored him, her focus on the phone in her hand as she headed to the kitchen.

"If you don't know who the father of your child is, then it could be anyone," Lincoln said, his words a challenge, meant to get under her skin.

Jo Lynn stopped in her tracks. She turned around, her eyes narrowing, a knowing smirk on her lips. "It could be you," she said quietly, but with enough weight behind it that Lincoln could feel the challenge in her voice.

Lincoln scoffed. "Not me. But you're the mother, and you don't even know who the father is?"

"I know who the father of my child is," Jo Lynn said, her voice stronger now.

"Then if you don't tell me, it must be the Father, because I don't understand the mystery," Lincoln muttered sarcastically.

Jo Lynn stared at him for a moment, confused. "My father?" she asked.

"Not your father, the priest," Lincoln corrected himself. "Is it your father's child?" He was genuinely curious now, but the high made him ask the question more boldly than he might have otherwise.

"No, idiot. He's not my father's son." Jo Lynn shook her head, a little offended now. "The biological father is a criminal, and I don't want him anywhere near my child, so I'd rather keep it a secret."

"A criminal?" Lincoln's voice was filled with disbelief. "What kind of criminal?"

Jo Lynn sighed, exasperated. "Lincoln, please, just drop it."

"No," Lincoln said, suddenly serious, wanting to know the gossip. "Now I really need to know. Is he in jail?"

"No, he's not in jail," Jo Lynn responded, but she seemed uncomfortable.

"Then where is he?" Lincoln demanded, stepping closer to her, unable to hide his curiosity.

"I don't know where he is, and he doesn't either..." Jo Lynn trailed off.

"Was it just a one-night stand?" Lincoln asked, his tone a little mocking.

"Maybe!" Jo Lynn said with a shrug, proud.

"You're a slut," Lincoln said, but his tone was playful.

"Excuse me! Are you judging me?" Jo Lynn retorted, her eyebrows raised, but she was smiling.

"Just fucking with you, *girl*. But seriously... is it hot, at laest?" Lincoln asked, trying to steer the conversation back.

"Yes, it was just a one-night stand, and yes, he was... is hot! But he's garbage, though... a criminal."

"What kind of criminal? You're killing me," he said, getting funny-anxious.

"A prostitute and a thief," Lincoln pressed, his curiosity getting the better of him.

"No shit. My father's son is a prostitute?" Lincoln almost laughed at the absurdity of it all.

"He's not his son. It's yours!" Jo Lynn clarified, her voice sharp.

"Okay, *mami*." Lincoln shrugged, but there was a sense of finality in his voice.

"I don't want my son to know," Jo Lynn said, her tone softening.

"He will never know," Lincoln promised, despite his ketamine haze.

"I could've aborted, you know," Jo Lynn said suddenly, her gaze intense as she looked at him.

"Thank God, you didn't," Lincoln replied, his voice a little more sincere now.

"God had nothing to with this. Thank you. You saved him. This is your son. Not his. Not anyone's. Yours!" Jo Lynn's voice trembled with emotion as she spoke the words.

"I promise, he will never know," Lincoln said, his voice firm, even though the drugs still clouded his thoughts.

"Show me his pictures," Lincoln asked, half-heartedly, but his curiosity was getting the best of him.

"I don't have his pics... oh, there should be..." Jo Lynn said, starting to look through her phone.

Sitting beside Jo Lynn, Lincoln watched her tap away on her phone. He saw her search for "Kenny Passeri" on Google, and the search results quickly populated the screen. The first link was an article from the *New York Times* titled: *"Kenny Passeri, The Most Expensive Escort in the World."* Jo Lynn clicked on it. His heart racing as the page loaded. The article detailed Derrick's story, accompanied by a photograph of him dressed in a black suit, leaving a New York City court with dark sunglasses and slicked-back hair. As Lincoln read, his breathing quickened, his mind struggling to stay calm. The story was so compelling, so daring, that he couldn't stop reading, even though the realization hit him like a punch to the gut. The article described how Derrick had been involved in a lawsuit, winning $1.5 million in a settlement with a prestigious law firm. The money had come from a Wall Street magnate for companionship services, but the money had been issued under false pretenses. Lincoln could hardly process the information, but he continued reading, unable to stop himself. Lincoln's mind raced as he read more, but his stomach churned. He felt nauseous and grabbed his phone, locking himself in the bathroom. Jo Lynn, unaware of his distress, remained in the other room, worried about his increasing *ketamine* use.

It took Lincoln longer than necessary to read the report detailing how Derrick's four lawyers had managed to win the lawsuit. The magnate had written a check for $1.5 million as a "donation" for a business project that never came to fruition. Social media had exploded with comments about the fraud, and Lincoln's mind couldn't make sense of it. His emotions, previously buried under the ketamine haze, began to rise to the surface. He cried, unable to hide his feelings, because when pain cuts deep, even the best of lovers can't escape its hold. Jo Lynn never saw him, as she was still in the bedroom while he pretended to be sick in the bathroom.

And when the night grew late, she entered the bathroom and found Lincoln asleep in the water. She shed her towel and slipped into the tub naked. Lincoln opened his eyes, exuding a sense of peace. When Jo Lynn sat in front of him, he looked at her, then carefully leaned over her belly and kissed it, showing love to the little one inside her. Jo Lynn ran her fingers through his dark hair with the full conviction that this was the man she wanted to spend the rest of her life with. Even though Jo Lynn wasn't religious, she wanted to be married by the time her child was born. At nine months pregnant, she finally decided to marry Lincoln, not just because she loved him desperately, but because he adored their unborn child irrationally, and for her, that was enough. Without him, she knew she would undoubtedly be a bad mother.

———

Jo Lynn's wedding dress was a gift from her father, but Lincoln's suit was a gift from her. When she took him to the designer's shop to have his measurements taken, Lincoln stepped out to visit the bathroom. Upon returning, he found Jo Lynn chatting with the designer, who, besides being talented, seemed to be a very close friend.

"And why are you here?" Lincoln asked challengingly as he walked toward them.

Jo Lynn, who knew him very well by then, realized he had taken *ketamine*, which explained his delay, and his erratic behavior.

"The bride shouldn't see the groom before the wedding," he said.

"That rule only applies to brides. There's no mystery in a black and white tailored suit, darling," Jo Lynn said, unaware of how humiliating her words might have been for the designer, who chose to remain silent.

"I'd prefer if you left," Lincoln admitted.

Jo Lynn didn't respond; she was more interested in hearing what he would say next.

"What does the lady want? What does the lady order?" He said, sarcastically.

Jo Lynn didn't feel intimidated because she didn't let herself be manipulated by people whose intelligence she considered inferior to hers, but she was annoyed. And when she got annoyed, she sometimes waited for those same people to reveal themselves, because it was anger that made them stupid, unlike her.

"...everything is as she wants it, when she wants it, isn't it, love?" Lincoln complained. "Lincoln, come here. Lincoln, do this, do that. Lincoln, give me. Lincoln, Lincoln, Lincoln. Is that how you told him to get you pregnant?"

Jo Lynn could've slapped his face, but instead, she grabbed her purse, gave the designer a kiss on the cheek, and left, fuming with anger, but silent. When they arrived home, Jo Lynn began throwing his clothes onto the floor, but Lincoln didn't care.

"How dare you humiliate me in front of everyone?" Jo Lynn shouted, her voice full of anger.

"It doesn't make sense what you're saying," Lincoln replied, his tone distant, trying to dismiss her anger.

"What doesn't make sense, Lincoln?" she insisted, moving closer, her frustration growing.

"You and Derrick!" He began, "If he's gay, how did you end up having sex with him?" Lincoln asked, his voice trembling with contained rage, as he looked at her with fierce intensity.

"Derrick, Derrick, Derrick. What's your obsession with him?" Jo Lynn responded, visibly exasperated.

"I want to know the truth," Lincoln demanded, his eyes fixed on hers, searching for any sign of doubt.

"What truth?" she asked, challenging him, though a shadow of exhaustion reflected in her tone.

"How'd you end up fucking him if he's gay?" Lincoln's voice shook, barely holding back rage.

Jo Lynn's jaw tightened. "Enough with Derrick," she snapped. "He's not gay; I've already told you."

"He is a fucking prostitute!" Lincoln shot out, stepping closer, his face inches from hers, daring her to react.

"He's not gay! I had him, not you," she shot back, her hands beginning to shake despite her forced calm.

"All the media says so. Are you blind, or can't you read?" Lincoln pressed, each word edged with bitterness as he closed the space between them.

"I'm not going to have this discussion with you right now," Jo Lynn said, stepping away from him, trying to maintain her dignity, though fear began to creep into her mind.

"Tell me," he demanded, gripping her arm, eyes wild with desperation.

"Lincoln!" she exclaimed, one hand resting on her belly in silent warning.

"Tell me, or you're going to drive me crazy," Lincoln squeezed harder, his desperation turning into blind fury.

"What do you want me to say?" she asked, her voice breaking under the pressure, fear mixing with anger.

"How did you end up fucking a gay man?" Lincoln spat, his voice loaded with jealousy and resentment, his eyes searching for answers in hers.

"Who would have thought you'd be so jealous?" Jo Lynn asked rhetorically, trying to maintain a facade of control, though inside she felt everything was falling apart.

"Did he kiss you while he fucked you?" Lincoln asked, his gaze full of pain as the words caught in his throat.

"Lincoln!" she exclaimed, alarmed by the crudeness of the question, feeling her heart pounding in her chest.

"Answer. Did he kiss you while he fucked you, yes or no?" Lincoln insisted, his voice trembling with fury, losing control.

"Yes, yes he kissed me," she admitted, with a mix of defiance and vulnerability in her tone.

"Did he spit in your mouth?" Lincoln continued, his voice turning into a whisper laced with venom, each word a dart aimed at her heart.

"No! Lincoln, stop it," Jo Lynn pleaded, her voice breaking, wishing it would all end.

"Then he didn't like you, I hope you know that," Lincoln said with a cruel tone, trying to hurt her deeply.

"I didn't expect him to like me. But do you like me?" she asked, pride dimmed to desperation.

"Not right now," Lincoln said, his voice cold, the distance between them insurmountable.

"You're sick in the head. You're jealous of a ghost. He doesn't exist, he only exists in your absurd imagination," Jo Lynn said, her voice full of despair, her words trying to be a shield against the pain.

"Where did you fuck him?" Lincoln asked, his voice now a sick whisper, each word a dagger.

"Stop, Lincoln," Jo Lynn pleaded, her voice breaking, fear beginning to take over her.

"Did you fuck him here," Lincoln pointed to the bed, "or did you fuck him in a bathroom?" Lincoln demanded, moving closer, his contained fury ready to explode.

"I fucked him there," she admitted, her tone changing, a twisted pride emerging from her despair, playing along with him.

"Where?" Lincoln pressed, his gaze fixed on her, demanding an answer.

"Enough," Jo Lynn said, trying to maintain some control, though she felt it slipping away.

"Answer the damn question, did you fuck him in this bed?" he pointed to the bed, his voice full of rage, his mind tangled in the torment of his own thoughts.

"I already told you I fucked him in the bed every time I wanted, until I got tired and threw him out. What more do you want to know?" she said, her voice now defiant and satisfied, each word a provocation.

"Is he better than me?" Lincoln asked, his voice trembling with rage.

"Much better than you," she replied, with calculated coldness.

Rabid, Lincoln grabbed her by the throat and squeezed. "But you're not better than me," he said, his voice a venomous whisper.

"What?" she asked, confused.

"Where did you meet him?" he cornered her, his voice cold and calculating.

"In the nightclub where I met you," she replied, defiant.

"You drugged him!" he accused, his voice full of contempt.

"There was no need, he was already drugged," she said, her voice firm.

"No, you drugged him and dragged him here," Lincoln replied, his voice full of fury.

"And I got my fill of him, just like I got my fill of you," she said, her voice full of defiance.

"You're a whore!" he said, squeezing her chin hard. Then he threw her onto the bed, savagely stripped her of her clothes, and used her as he pleased. Although she resisted at first, in the end, she let herself be abused. But when she decided to stop him, she did it with the same fierceness that characterized her, getting out of bed and walking toward the bathroom.

"I'm not done," he shouted, dissatisfied.

Jo Lynn locked herself in the bathroom, slamming the door with force. She sat on the toilet, thoughtful, deciding how to feel, whether she was sexually abused or not.

Irritated, Lincoln noticed that he had run out of *ketamine*. Desperate, he began looking through the pockets of his jackets, pants, and even the insides of his shoes. After tearing through everything, he searched for the key to unlock the bottom drawer of his nightstand, but when he couldn't find it, he broke in, revealing a collection of about twenty journals inside. He took them out one by one, flipping through the pages until the gram bag of ketamine fell out. With the urgency of an ambulance, he inhaled the powder deeply, which sent him into a momentary state of intoxication where he began to write furiously in one of his journals, his mind detaching from time and space. He collapsed onto the bed and began an intimate interaction with the sheets, the same sheets where Derrick had once lain, and came on. And in the euphoria of that hallucinatory moment, he felt as if he were becoming pregnant with the man, whom he could die for.

———

Lincoln married in black, not just because he was the groom, but because on that gray day, he was mourning on the inside. Jo Lynn married in white, not just because she was the bride, but because on that gray day, it was the happiest day of her life. With what Jo Lynn's father spent on her wedding dress, he could have fed more than a thousand people for a month. The reason he spent such a sum was because he wouldn't be attending the wedding, and he didn't want to hear complaints for the rest of his days. Besides, he had devised an insurance policy to protect the investment in case the marriage didn't work out. To protect his daughter's interests, without her knowing, he had her sign a prenup along with the delivery documents for the wedding dress. He knew she'd be so excited that she would sign anything just to be alone with her dress. Despite being nearly nine months pregnant, Jo Lynn married in an opulent wedding gown featuring a bra covered in diamonds, supporting a pair of breasts that looked like two juicy, freshly cut melons. The voluminous skirt extended into a long, flowing train, creating a majestic and regal presence.

Lincoln and Jo Lynn were married on a cold Sunday afternoon at *San Nicholas of Tolentine Church* in Atlantic City. And although they appeared happy in the photos, the reality was quite different. Lincoln had consumed so much ketamine that he was no longer himself, and if he smiled, it was only out of reflex. In a desperate attempt to keep him conscious, Jo Lynn forced him to take cocaine so he wouldn't fall asleep. But her efforts didn't free her from the weariness and frustration she felt, because in addition to taking care of Lincoln, she could no longer bear the heavy belly she carried, as if she were lugging a sack of stones that could fall between her legs at any moment. They couldn't even attend their own reception, as Lincoln was so intoxicated that, at the altar, just before saying "I do," his knees buckled and he collapsed to the floor, unconscious as a rag. Jo Lynn wasn't surprised. After moments of silence, she knelt by Lincoln's side, her movements mechanical, helping him up and guiding him out. She ignored the guests' murmurs, her face set with practiced composure. As they got into the car, leaving the guests behind to imagine countless scenarios, none of them suspected that the combination of ketamine and GBL was responsible for such a disaster on what was supposed to be a special day. With almost calculated coldness, Jo Lynn ordered the driver to take them to the hotel instead of the hospital.

In the hotel room, Lincoln slept for a couple of hours while Jo Lynn sat beside him, unmoving, her mind tangled in thoughts that began and ended with her mother. Her gaze seemed lost, but inside, a mix of fury and sadness kept her on edge. When Lincoln finally woke up, he gave a weak smile from his pillow. It took Lincoln a few seconds to remember what had happened, and shame hit him like a slap in the face.

"Are you mad?" he asked, his voice tinged with guilt.

"How do you feel?" she asked, with concern, though her voice betrayed a growing distance.

"I have a surprise for you," he said, trying to inject some enthusiasm into the conversation.

"Another one?" she responded, her calm masking her annoyance. "We can't go on like this, Lincoln. We need help."

"Once our baby is born, everything will be fine. I won't be able to..." he hesitated before correcting himself, "I won't have time for nonsense. You know kids take up a lot of time, right?"

Jo Lynn nodded, but the worry still showed in her eyes, though she forced a smile.

"I promise, okay?" Lincoln said, with a coddling expression, trying to break her resistance.

"Do you love me?" she asked, her voice filled with fear.

"Not more than our child, but more than my own life, that's for sure," he replied, looking her in the eyes with a sincerity that only he knew either was genuine or not. Then, he sat up on the bed and kissed her passionately, making Jo Lynn's tears start to fall.

Lincoln, remembering Derrick, wiped her tears with his tongue, just as Derrick had done to him back when he was still happy.

"Lincoln!" she exclaimed, disgusted and confused. But he continued, licking her face until the situation turned into a strange, still playful game. Jo Lynn, despite her initial resistance, eventually gave in to the intensity of the moment.

Just then, a phone call came in on Lincoln's phone.

"The surprise is here," he said, excited.

She smiled, convinced that everything that had happened that day had been worth it.

"Go into the bathroom, and come out when I tell you, okay?" he asked, with a mix of seriousness and excitement.

Jo Lynn sighed deeply and headed to the bathroom, unable to stop herself from wondering what else she could expect from this strange night. Upon entering the bathroom, Jo Lynn was met with her reflection in the mirror. Unlike other times, this time she had the moment to truly take herself in, and she recalled her slender figure before the pregnancy made her feel as if she were carrying a chronic disease. Seeing herself in the dress, she remembered her father, her parents, but it was an illusion because she hadn't been able to stop thinking about them all day. Although she didn't admit that she missed him, she made a call, fully intending not to cause any drama over his absence.

"Dad!" she exclaimed, her voice vibrating with contained emotion.

"Sorry for not calling you earlier," her father's voice sounded distant, but warm.

"It's okay, Dad," she responded, her voice trembling slightly, lying to both him and herself.

"I hope you're happy, because that dress cost me a fortune."

"You're so silly, Dad. The dress has nothing to do with my happiness." Her father laughed heartily.

"Women! If I hadn't bought you that dress, you'd be bombarding me like your mother, saying I'm a cheapskate."

The conversation was interrupted by a knock on the door, along with Lincoln's concerned voice from outside, accompanied by the ascending pulsating beats of electronic music.

"My love, is everything okay?" he asked.

"Is that him?" her father interrupted with an accusatory tone.

"How old is he? Fourteen?"

"Goodbye, Dad," she said abruptly before hanging up.

"Yes, love, I just need a minute," she replied to Lincoln, her voice barely audible over the music.

"Take your time... I love you," Lincoln's words carried an enthusiasm that resonated strangely in the small bathroom space. Approaching the closed door, and through the crack of the door frame, she whispered a response she knew he wouldn't hear: "I love you, too."

Hesitantly, Jo Lynn dialed her mother's number, only to be directed straight to voicemail.

"Mom?" she began, her voice trembling and filled with fading hope. "Hi, Mom... I got married today. Well, you already know that." Jo Lynn paused, swallowing hard, her eyes fixated on her reflection. "Mom?... I thought you'd come." She faltered, regaining composure. "But you're hard and cruel. I despise you." Her voice, filled with repressed anger, broke through the silence, echoing against the bathroom walls. Tears quickly welled up in her eyes, reflecting a deep pain beyond mere sadness.

"I didn't call to complain, but... I'm a married woman now, and I know you don't believe he loves me, but he does... he shows me every day. He's a good man, not like Dad, not like him," she paused, pulling the phone away as she struggled to control her emotions, feeling how each word weighed heavier than the last. "You had to see the wedding dress; it's so beautiful that even a fat girl would look regal; I could live in it forever, Mom," looking at the massive dress in the mirror, her voice cracked, making it evident how hard it was to continue.

"I'm sorry, I've been crying a lot lately; out of happiness, of course, though it's still embarrassing," she lied again, but this time forced a smile through her tears. "I'm so happy... I'm so happy that I wish you had come, at least for the photos... I wish we could have those memories together... Sorry, Mom, I'm very sentimental; well, you know, it must be the overweight."

Quickly, she composed herself upon seeing her reflection in the mirror and feeling hypocritical talking to the void.

"What were you doing, huh? What was more important today than coming to my wedding? Why wouldn't you want to be with me on what's supposed to be the most important day in a woman's life?" Her anger built as she raised her voice.

"Why weren't you there for me, holding my hand, fixing my hair, or just doing nothing as usual? You're hard and cruel, you're a repulsive human being, and I despise you. I hate you, Hartford. I hate you for being my mother, and I hate myself for being your daughter. I hope you suffer when you die," through uncontrollable sobs, she repeatedly smashed her phone against the marble sink until it stopped working, and when there was nothing left, she collapsed to the floor, consumed by the same pain that had plagued her all her life.

Outside the bathroom, the night descended beyond the horizon, illuminating the room through the windows and casting a tapestry of shadows while neon lights and circuit music painted the suite with vibrant tones. The nightstand told a story of excess: traces of *ketamine*, an amber bottle of GBL, lubricant, and poppers... lay scattered, testifying to the chaotic indulgence that dominated the space. A man named Dante, with the allure of James Dean, was taking Lincoln from behind without restraint. Lincoln, his eyes closed but visibly in ecstasy, responded eagerly to the sexual pleasure being bestowed upon him. Dante was one of those men who grew more beautiful the more serious they became, but when high, he transformed into something akin to a puppy. When he saw Jo Lynn standing in the bathroom doorway like a zombie, in her long wedding dress and smeared makeup from crying so much, he said, "Hey!"

"Don't stop," Lincoln implored.

"Lincoln!" Jo Lynn shouted, furious.

It took Lincoln only a fraction of a second to stand in front of his wife, pretending to be concerned for her.

"Is everything okay, baby?" Lincoln asked, grabbing her face as he struggled to keep his eyes open and his knees steady.

Jo Lynn held back her rage, assessing his critical state of intoxication.

"The surprise I told you about. Derrick is here!"

"Derrick?" Jo Lynn asked, offended.

"Not Derrick. What's your name?" Lincoln asked.

"Dante."

"Dante, Dante, big penis, he's here to make you happy."

"You're a faggot!" Jo Lynn exclaimed, wounded.

Lincoln snapped to attention, offended.

"No! What are you talking about?" he said, scared. "I'm not a faggot. This is a surprise for you, love. Derrick, come here!"

"His name is Dante, *not* Derrick," Jo Lynn shouted.

"Stop confusing me!" Lincoln shouted at Jo Lynn. "I said Derrick... Dante," he corrected himself, "I said Dante," desperate, confused, exposed. "Dante, come over here and touch my wife," he ordered.

Dante approached with the intention to touch her with his hands and the charm of his soul.

"Don't you dare to touch me!"

Dante stepped back.

Jo Lynn looked at Lincoln with contempt, analyzing how dangerous, deceitful, enveloping, and manipulative he was. Even she hadn't dared go this far during the days of Pablo Episcopal.

"You never loved me," she confessed painfully. "It's Derrick's child you love, not mine, not me," she shot back, watching as Lincoln's confidence crumbled.

"I love you. I love you with all my life."

"Shut up. Just shut up; I know everything. I know he used you, then left you, and now all you're left with are your stupid love poems." She screamed at his face.

Lincoln had never been more awake than in that moment, stunned and exposed.

"Men like him don't fall in love with men like you, Lincoln. So even if you were reborn, he wouldn't notice you, and if you don't believe me, just look at yourself in the mirror." She added.

"He did love me; he just never knew it because I never told him," Lincoln confessed in a painful moment of sincerity.

"I did love you." She said, painfully broken.

"But I didn't," he replied coldly, something he wouldn't have said if he hadn't been under the influence.

In a fit of rage, Jo Lynn grabbed the corded phone on the night table and smashed it against

Lincoln's head, knocking him unconscious with the first blow. Dante, with his hands over his mouth, stood frozen in shock, staring at her. Jo Lynn walked out of the room with the phone in her hands, as if her soul had betrayed her and left her alone. It took Lincoln a few seconds to come to his senses, and when he woke up, he saw Dante trying to revive him. As he sat up, he felt the blood begin to trickle down his forehead; his head throbbed with pain.

"Where is she?" he asked Dante, disoriented.

"She left. Lincoln, can you pay me now?" Dante responded, impatient.

"Not now," Lincoln replied, struggling to stand up.

"I need my money now," Dante insisted, annoyed.

"Are you blind? Can't you see what's happening?" Lincoln shouted at him. "I'll pay you, but not right now. Wait here or do whatever you want," he said as he quickly put some clothes on, and hurried out, blood running down his head and dripping from his forehead. As he left the room, he found himself in a long hallway he didn't remember seeing before. At the end of the corridor, in front of the elevator, he found the abandoned corded phone, got into the elevator and descended to the lobby. Downstairs, everything seemed to be running normally, as if no one had witnessed a woman possessed by rage, on the verge of a nervous breakdown, wearing a wedding dress with nine months of pregnancy and smeared makeup. Only an eight-year-old boy, who still seemed to be in shock, stood there with a melting ice cream in his hand, his small mind trying to comprehend the mystery of the woman, an image he would never forget. When the boy and Lincoln locked eyes, the blood streaming down Lincoln's forehead didn't scare him, but it did hint at the marital drama. Instinctively, the boy pointed towards the door. Lincoln winked at him, thinking it would be a kind gesture, but in reality, with his bloodied face, it came off more like a scene from a horror movie. Outside the hotel, the dark night stretched out, with thick storm clouds hiding the moon and stars, allowing only a faint light that barely illuminated the turbulent sea, where large waves clashed violently. Lincoln stepped out into the street, but there was no sign of Jo Lynn. Despite calling her name, a deep instinct pulled him toward the beach. And there, in his agony, alone with the sea, the sky, and who brought him there, he plunged into the ocean, searching for what life had already given him, but which he had lost in his attempt to capture another love story in a single moment.

DOWN UNDERGROUND

*"I'm so happy because today I found my
friends—they're in my head."* Kurt Cobain

It was an unusually quiet night at the Atlantic
City Regional Medical Center, so calm and dark
that it felt more haunted than the little pointed-
roof house at the end of the world. The clock
struck 10 p.m. when Lincoln, saltier than the sea
and reeking of fish, stood alone in the hallway,
his bare feet damp and sandy. His gaze was fixed
ahead, guilt pressing down like the blood-soaked
bandage wrapped around his head. At 10:10
p.m., Lincoln's thoughts drifted to ketamine,
the one thing that could cut through the haze
of uncertainty gnawing at his sanity. His fingers
trembled as they searched the wet pockets of his
pants, desperate for a small miracle. But there
was nothing—only the fine, unforgiving sand of
the sea. By 10:12 p.m., Lincoln's thoughts had
spiraled into a singular, overpowering need. His

hands shook as his mind latched onto the familiar escape that *ketamine* promised. It wasn't just a craving; it was a gnawing hunger that clawed at his insides, demanding release. He could almost feel the dissociation, that sweet numbness lifting him out of his skin, dulling the sharp edges of reality. The weight of the world, the crushing pressure in his chest, the relentless storm of regrets... all of it needed to dissolve, drawn into the immediate miracle that *ketamine* offered. His mouth dried at the thought, his fingers twitching with anticipation. He could almost taste the metallic tang in the back of his throat, the prelude to that blessed disconnect. The craving wasn't just in his mind—it was in his bones, a deep, aching hunger. Every second without it was unbearable, every breath too heavy, too urgent. He needed to float, to lose himself in that void where nothing could touch him, where the world would finally quiet, and his thoughts would find peace. At 10:15 p.m., Lincoln noticed the doctor's silhouette approaching, cradling a newborn in his arms.

"No!" Lincoln cried, tears streaming down his face as he fell to his knees, arms outstretched in rejection.

The doctor stepped closer.

"Lincoln, look at your son."

"No! Take him away, please," Lincoln pleaded.

"Take him where, Lincoln?" the doctor asked, his voice gentle yet firm.

"Take him away, please... he's not my son," Lincoln cried, his voice breaking, his knees and elbows sinking into the cold, sterile floor as his face fell into his hands.

"Lincoln, stop. Don't say that. He can hear you."

The doctor knelt beside him, gently lifting Lincoln's head so he could see the baby. But Lincoln refused to look, even when the baby began to make soft, innocent sounds.

"Your father loves you very much. Just wait until he sees those big *blue* eyes," the doctor cooed, caressing the baby. "Where did you get those big blue eyes from?"

"Blue?" Lincoln asked, his voice trembling as memories of Derrick's large, blue eyes flooded his mind. Fearfully, he looked at his son for the first time. And though the baby wasn't made of *ketamine*, he brought an unexpected surge of joy to Lincoln, a joy that blossomed as he imagined Derrick by his side, proud and happy to see that his son had inherited his own big blue eyes. Lincoln reached out and took the baby into his arms, holding him close, and in the warmth of his thoughts about Derrick, he shielded the baby from the world.

———

At the funeral home, Jo Lynn's body lay in a glass casket, just as she had asked her father when she was nine years old, after discovering the fascinating Snow White casket. Meanwhile,

Lincoln, his head bandaged from the blows Jo Lynn had inflicted with the telephone cord, sat in a deserted area at the back, reserved only for employees. In his arms, he held his newborn baby, neglected in a position where its neck would be seriously compromised if one of Lincoln's fingers lost strength or slipped. Next to him, Santiago was absorbed in his cellphone, entertaining himself with video games. Suddenly, the distant sound of heels clicking against the floor began to approach through the wide hallway of tiles. From the sound, Lincoln recognized her. During those days of supposed mourning, Hartford had decided to dress in black, adorning her head with a hat that draped a veil over her face. Her intention was to prevent people from criticizing her appearance if her look seemed too fresh, because, as the mother of the deceased, people absurdly take pleasure in seeing her look like a poorly made eyesore. Hartford wasn't as wicked as Jo Lynn claimed; in fact, she saw herself as a woman grateful for life. On the day of her daughter's wedding, which tragically coincided with her death, Hartford was on her way to Los Angeles for an appointment with a famous plastic surgeon, an appointment that had taken her six months to secure. Upon landing in Los Angeles and hearing about the tragedy that had struck her daughter, she was relieved that Jo Lynn hadn't died before she left New York; canceling such an important appointment for a life already lost would have been, for her, another major catastrophe.

"The mother drowns, and the child ends up with a broken neck," she remarked while watching her grandson, carelessly held in Lincoln's arms, who, lost in his stupor, had forgotten to adjust the baby's position. From her purse, Hartford pulled out a $100 bill and handed it to Santiago, who looked at her with a mix of admiration and curiosity.

"Go get us a couple of coffees," she ordered.

"The coffee here is free," Santiago pointed out, while Lincoln watched the scene in silence.

"Take the money, leave us alone and don't bring anything."

Santiago, puzzled, took the bill and left.

As she observed Lincoln's disheveled appearance, his bleary eyes and trembling hands clinging to his infant son, Hartford couldn't suppress a flicker of disgust. She would have despised Lincoln's spiral, but even more so, she despised that her family's reputation was now tied to it. She sat down next to Lincoln and studied her grandson carefully.

"What name are you going to give him?" she asked.

"Kenny."

"Kenneth!"

"Kenny, his name is Kenny."

"Kenny isn't a name, it's a diminutive. If you call him Kenny, you'll be setting him up with serious perception issues that he'll have to deal with for the rest of his life."

"What do you want, Hartford?" Lincoln replied, tired of her dismissing his choice.

135

Offended by his tone, Hartford opened her *Chanel* purse and pulled out a small golden box, the size of a matchbox, containing white powder. Lincoln's eyes lit up at the sight of it, and she, noticing his reaction, offered him the cocaine. Lincoln, feeling a mix of shame and guilt, refused.

"Please, Lincoln, don't be ridiculous," she said, dismissing his shame. "You've done it for less noble reasons."

Outwardly, Lincoln pretended to hesitate, but inside, he had already inhaled every last particle of that potion that brought him back to life, leaving him momentarily numb like a pane of glass. Hartford wasn't a bad woman, but in the self-discoveries she hadn't yet come to terms with, she found a strange pleasure in watching others' decline; the deeper the fall, the more fortunate she felt in her own rise. Seeing Lincoln consume the cocaine for the first time gave her a subtle satisfaction, though she kept it contained, knowing that no enemy is too small.

"And you?" he asked, annoyed, seeing her put the box back in her *Chanel* purse.

"What kind of mother would I be?" she replied rhetorically, with the firm intention of making him feel as useless as a pinky toe.

Lincoln felt like what he feared most: a drug addict, and though he wanted to say something, he found silence the best way not to reveal his truth.

"It must be very hard to believe you have everything one day, and the next realize you never had anything," she said with cold satisfaction, enjoying the effect of her words.

"I'm very lucky," he responded with an ironic smile, knowing his words would irritate her.

"Lucky?"

He nodded, confusing her. She waited for him to continue, but he remained silent just to annoy her.

"What makes you lucky?" she finally asked.

"Everything," he said, studying her. "Family," he added, enjoying the confusion on her face.

"Jo Lynn mentioned you were an orphan," she observed coolly, her gaze assessing him as if appraising merchandise.

"Not anymore," he said, meeting her gaze. "Now I have you," he added, watching how she feigned a smile while internally recoiling.

Hartford would have preferred to be burned alive rather than accept a *charro* as part of her family, but from her ex-husband, she learned that the most important thing in any business is the talent for storytelling.

"Of course, we're a family that sticks together, and we want the best for you and your son," she began. "My ex-husband and I have discussed your situation and believe that, being so young, you should return to university, study, and prepare yourself. You could even work in one of our companies."

This was a move by Hartford that Lincoln hadn't anticipated, and although it contradicted Jo Lynn's explicit version of her mother, he quickly got carried away by vivid images of himself going to university without finishing school, working in an office, and finally building a life of his own.

"We have an apartment in Los Angeles. You could live there, and we'll provide you with a car to get around. My ex-husband also has offices there, where you could start working right away."

"I've never been to Los Angeles," he said, concerned.

"Los Angeles is like a big *town*, and *your* people are all there," she said with a casual tone that sounded racist.

"My people are here," he shot back, offended. "And honestly, I'd rather raise my son here in New York."

"We'll give your son up for adoption, so we'll see about that."

"Excuse me?" he pretended not to have heard her clearly.

"Lincoln, it must be illegal for you to raise children," she said sarcastically. "How old are you?"

"If I could make a child, I can raise him."

"That's debatable. You've been lucky so far, but Jo Lynn is gone, and we have no responsibility for you or your son."

"My son has *rights*."

"Your son will have the rights his parents can provide. And as far as I know, on one side, you have nothing, and on the other, Jo Lynn is dead. If she never worked a day in her life, I doubt she left anything to inherit to you or your son, only debts. But don't worry about that; I can take care of them unless you insist."

"Jo Lynn wouldn't have wanted you to adopt her child."

"We both know Jo Lynn didn't want him, and if she had him, it was because of you," she began. "What I still don't understand is why, in these new circumstances, you still want him when, at your age and with the opportunities available to you, you could have a much better life without him," she said with coldness and uncertainty.

"Because he's my son."

"And this is your life, so you decide how to live it," she added with a mix of impatience and disdain. "Think about it, but if you don't take our offer, don't count on us."

She stood up and, in Lincoln's free hand, mysteriously placed the golden box of cocaine. Lincoln, feeling the shape of the box, recognized it instantly. When he looked at it, stunned, he found a complicit Hartford, who winked at him. Then, with the tips of her fingers, she pretended to touch Kenny's little nose in a motion that mimicked a gentle wave, and left. Lincoln quickly put away in his pockets the little golden cocaine box.

———

Since Jo Lynn's death, Santiago took care of Kenny. Although Lincoln pretended to be interested in learning how to be a father, with each passing day, he seemed less like a person and more like a bundle of chaos. Santiago, understanding his pain, avoided interfering in Lincoln's activities: sleeping during the day and locking himself in the bathroom at night to smoke methamphetamine behind Santiago's back. It wasn't out of fear that Santiago didn't intervene in this *destructive* routine, but because Lincoln had developed a bitterness that manifested in aggressive and disdainful behavior.

One night after midnight, Lincoln stumbled out of the bathroom, naked and unsteady, trying not to make noise. He slid under the sheets, positioning himself behind Santiago, who, after so many sleepless nights, had finally fallen asleep. If Lincoln hadn't hugged him tightly while shivering with cold, Santiago might not have woken up, but feeling Lincoln's agitated breath on his neck, he woke abruptly.

"Lincoln?" he turned to look at him, annoyed.

It was evident that Lincoln was in a state of euphoria and visibly aroused. Santiago jumped out of bed, offended. Lincoln, displaying an absurd sense of freedom, stretched out on the bed, biting his lips as he enjoyed the sacred effect of the drugs he had consumed.

"What are you doing?" Santiago asked, disgusted.

Lincoln felt sexy and liberated, but the image he projected was quite gross and disturbing: so sweaty he looked like a pig, so pale like paper, and with dark circles the size of the moon.

"What does it look like I'm doing?" Lincoln responded lightly and shamelessly, licking his lips. Of all the things he could desire at that moment, he only wanted one, and it was right in front of him. In a swift movement, Santiago, feeling second-hand embarrassment, covered him with the sheets.

"Time to sleep."

"To hell with sleep," Lincoln said, throwing off the sheets. "Come here," he invited, moving closer.

"Lincoln, enough already," Santiago replied, covering Lincoln's private parts with the sheet. "If you could see how ridiculous you look, you wouldn't be making such a distasteful spectacle."

"I don't want to sleep, and I don't wanna see how ridiculous I look," Lincoln raised his voice, tossing aside the sheets with one hand while grabbing Santiago's arm with the other, pulling him closer.

Santiago pushed him, throwing him back onto the bed.

"You're sick! You need *Jesus Christ!*" he shouted.

"I need a *man...* that´s what I need. What are you, and what are you gonna do about it?" Lincoln shouted back.

"You're using that crap, aren't you?" Santiago said, furious. "Is that what's got you acting like an idiot?" he asked, so angry he almost hit him, but instead headed to the bathroom. Inside, he found the mess: white towels strewn across the damp floor and the counter cluttered with personal care products mixed with recreational drugs in various forms: powders, pills, capsules, and a lighter. Santiago grabbed the lighter as evidence that Lincoln had been smoking, and with even greater anger, began searching the lower cabinet under the sink. Realizing he'd been exposed, Lincoln pushed him and slammed the cabinet shut. Santiago, stronger, grabbed Lincoln by the neck and moved him aside as if he were a chess piece. He quickly opened the cabinet and found the infamous pipe, the size of a forearm, loaded with meth crystals. Without thinking, he smashed it against the wall. Lincoln, in shock, knelt in front of the shattered pieces of the pipe.

"Get out of my house!" he shouted, hurt, as if someone had broken his son's bones. Santiago didn't respond, nor did he bend down to pick up the broken pieces. When Lincoln turned toward the door, he saw that Santiago was already gone. He stood up and ran to the living room, where he found Santiago getting dressed.

"I'm sorry, I'm sorry, please don't leave, don't leave me here alone, please," he begged, trying to stop Santiago from putting on his clothes.

"Move!" Santiago said, short-tempered.

Lincoln insisted.

Santiago, with a shove, threw him to the floor, left.

Lincoln got up and ran to the door.

"Santiago! Don't ever come back, you hear me?" he shouted, furious, as Santiago disappeared into the elevator.

As Lincoln slammed the door shut, he thought for a moment that he was left alone, but Kenny's cries spreading through the air reminded him otherwise, signaling the beginning of a night that promised to be as long as a nightmare. Since Kenny's birth, Lincoln hadn't had the chance to care for him alone. Approaching the crib, he played circuit music from his phone. It quickly started to echo through the speakers, strategically placed around the *loft*, drowning out the decibels of Kenny's cries. Then, he took him in his arms and, like a game or a challenge, a result of his intoxication, began to spin on his feet at a dizzying speed.

———

On another of the many sleepless nights, after having smoked for hours, but tired of Kenny, who insisted on crying and not sleeping, Lincoln tried to feed him, but it wasn't hunger. He wrapped him up, but it wasn't cold. Kenny missed the warmth of Santiago's side. Lincoln's arms, shaky and disoriented, only increased Kenny's confusion and anxiety. Desperate, Lincoln sent text messages to Santiago, but they went unanswered. Santiago was deeply offended, not only for being thrown out but also for the sexual harassment he had not yet overcome. In a desperate act, Lincoln had an idea to calm Kenny's cries, which were becoming unbearable alongside his already existing depressive episode. He went to the kitchen and, with trembling hands, prepared the bottle. He added ten drops of GBL—the same liquid that helped him sleep deeply, and the same liquid that had been used to sedate him the night he was abused. Within seconds, Kenny fell deeply asleep. Although his night no longer belonged to his son, he found no comfort either because the methamphetamine not only kept him awake but also started to play tricks on him. Suddenly, he began to hear strange sounds, like distant heels coming from the living room. He went out to investigate, but there was no one there. Then he heard the same heels approaching the main door. Cautiously, he approached and looked through the peephole, but there was also no one outside. He began to sweat cold as the sound of the heels echoed closer and closer. Unable to see anything, fear overcame him, and he ran to hide under the bed where his son still slept deeply. The sound of the heels was approaching the room, and Lincoln, his face drenched in sweat, recognized Hartford's *Chanel* heels. He immediately crawled out from under the bed.

"What are you doing here?" he asked irritably. However, when he came out, there was no one there.

"Hartford?" he shouted, confused, while Kenny remained lost in a deep sleep.

Suddenly, his phone rang, and without looking at the screen, he answered randomly.

"Hartford, what do you want?" he asked, irritated.

Hartford was at a resort in Hawaii, enjoying herself with her friends, who had decided on a well-deserved vacation to clear Hartford's mind after the sudden death of her only daughter. And although Hartford often wore heels, she wasn't thinking about Lincoln at all—but her lawyers were.

Laurie Anderson, a young lawyer with great promise in the legal world, looked barely thirty despite being thirty-six. Her radiant skin reflected her disciplined lifestyle: she didn't drink alcohol, had never tried drugs, and had no children or a lover interested in starting a family. Her strict and healthy routine made her an impeccable judge of those whose lives were slipping through their fingers, and she felt an infinite pity for them.

Laurie sat by the window in a café, a block from Lincoln's loft. She waited there, unhurried, but as time passed, she began to feel irritated and disrespected. She decided to call Lincoln, who hadn't responded to any of her text messages.

"Hartford, what the hell do you want? What are you doing at my house?" Lincoln answered irritably, caught in a paranoid episode induced by methamphetamine use.

"Lincoln?" Laurie responded, confused. "This is Laurie Anderson, from the Vanderbilt law firm. We had a meeting at two this afternoon at the café a block from your place," she said, instinctively glancing at her watch, which read nearly 2:30. "What time do you think you'll arrive?" she asked cautiously, trying not to sound annoyed.

Lincoln, having completely forgotten the meeting, hurriedly hung up, threw on some pants, and left his loft with half of his face covered by a black hoodie, forgetting to check on his still-sleeping son. When he arrived at the café, Lincoln quickly identified Laurie; of all the women there, she was the only one who seemed uncomfortable in her tailored office suit. Lincoln sat down across from her, wiped the sweat from his forehead with his hand, then dried his damp hands on his hoodie before extending one to her. Laurie hesitated to respond to the gesture, but in that situation, she found no other genuine way to greet him, so she shook his hand, although she discreetly wiped it under the table with the thick fabric of her skirt, which felt like it was made of carpet. It was the first time she had seen him, and she immediately noticed the toll his excesses had taken: enlarged pores, deep circles under his eyes, and significant loss of skin elasticity. She also detected a characteristic smell, a mixture of dirt and accumulated sweat, convincing her that Lincoln hadn't bathed in several days. Moreover, she observed that his mental state was altered by the strange way he looked around, emanating an uncomfortable sense of paranoia. Although she couldn't pinpoint the exact reasons, she suspected he was under the influence of some substance.

"Mr. Lincoln, it's 3 p.m.," Laurie said, with a tone of slight complaint.

"Do you have kids?" he asked brazenly.

"No, I don't have children," she replied, offended by the question.

"If you did, you wouldn't be so upset. Look, I don't want to waste your time, and I'm not going to pretend that you care about my well-being or that you're on my side. But I'm not going to give my son up for adoption, I won't move to Los Angeles, and I'm certainly not leaving our home."

Laurie was surprised by how straightforward Lincoln was about something that had taken her hours to plan how to address.

"When you mention 'our home,' are you referring to the loft?" she asked, already knowing the answer.

Lincoln nodded.

"That apartment never belonged to Jo Lynn, not even to her father. That property is Hartford's. It's thanks to her that you and your son are still living there..."

The news hit Lincoln like a bucket of cold water. In his daydreams, he had planned to raise Kenny there without ever considering that living in such a luxurious building would cost far more than he had in his bank accounts, which he still had access to.

"Jo Lynn was never your wife," Laurie pressed, her tone calm but firm. "You lost consciousness before saying 'I do'—there's no legal union."

"She's my wife, and Kenny's my son," Lincoln snapped, his voice trembling with conviction.

"There are videos and testimonies that say otherwise," Laurie clarified, maintaining her composure.

Lincoln remained silent for a moment. Sitting across from Laurie and staring at her intently, he tried to recall that fateful day.

Laurie noticed his confusion and took advantage of the pause to pull a check from her purse. With a calculated move, she slid it across the table, placing it face down in front of Lincoln, resting her hand on it.

"Without a marriage, you have no legal protection to stay in the US," she added, satisfied.

"My son is American," Lincoln responded with an empowered smile, shaking his head, incredulous but not surprised, as expected, at his in-laws' gesture of sending him a check.

"With all due respect, Lincoln, but there are also rumors that you're not the father."

Lincoln slammed the table so hard that everyone there looked at them.

"Kenny is my son, and if anyone dares to touch him..."

"No one will touch him without your consent," Laurie interrupted, revealing the check.

Lincoln took it urgently, and as he counted the zeros, he paused, momentarily confused by the amount.

"What's this?" Lincoln retorted, offended.

"It's nothing more than a gift."

"You're all monsters. You want to get rid of my son, just like you got rid of my Jo Lynn."

"No one got rid of Jo Lynn, Lincoln. She drowned. It was an accident. Or wasn't it? You should know. Weren't you there?" Laurie asked, with a cynical tone.

Lincoln let out a sarcastic sigh at the insinuation.

"Go to hell and tell them my son won't be adopted," he ordered as he pocketed the check. Then, he stood up abruptly and leaned over Laurie, forcing her to lean back, intimidated, clutching the chair tightly. "And also tell them that I'd rather slit his throat myself than hand him over to them," he threatened in a low, satisfied, and menacing voice.

Laurie felt a knot in her stomach as the situation slipped from her control. Although she usually remained calm in tense situations, the desperation of not being able to convince Lincoln and seeing him determined to leave made her react instinctively. She jumped up, her heart pounding.

"Do you really think he'll be okay with you? Look at yourself; you're not well," she said, trying to keep her composure as the murmurs in the café died down and all eyes fixed on the tense confrontation unfolding before them. Even so, her voice didn't waver.

"I am his father," he said proudly. "And if they want to have him, adopt him, or do God knows what to him, they'll have to kill me first."

Lincoln rushed out of the café, driven by fury and haunted by the demons that had led him to this point. The sound of the door slamming behind him echoed in the quiet café, and Laurie stood there, feeling the weight of her failure. She knew that convincing Lincoln to see reason was going to be much harder than she had anticipated, and from the window, witnessed Lincoln entering into the bank across the street.

Westerners could never quite pinpoint the exact origin of Ju-Yin's striking features, but the Easterners knew she was from China. Socially, Ju-Yin was bold and outgoing, a magnetic presence at any gathering, but behind her desk, she transformed into a composed lady with nails impeccably painted in cherry red. Her hands, always moisturized, left a cold, clean, and creamy sensation when touched. From her glass office, Ju-Yin watched as Lincoln rushed in. With a sense of anticipation, she headed to her office door, suspecting something wasn't right with him.

"Can I help you?" Ju-Yin asked, maintaining a polite distance, her voice carrying a practiced warmth. She noted Lincoln's rapid approach and the agitation in his gaze, the kind of behavior she knew to approach cautiously.

"I want you to open a new account for me, take my money from my old account, and move it to my new account," he demanded, gesticulating with his hands as if the words were slipping out before he could organize them. He fell silent, questioning whether he had made himself clear.

Ju-Yin understood perfectly, but Lincoln's anxiety caught her attention. Something in his behavior didn't add up. "Of course, did you bring your ID?" she asked as she calmly walked to her desk, maintaining a composed demeanor. Lincoln followed closely, almost invading her personal space.

"No, but I know my full name," he replied, almost defiantly, as if that should be enough.

Ju-Yin sat behind her desk, her composure unbroken. She noticed Lincoln's hands trembling slightly. "I'll need your physical ID," she clarified, keeping her tone steady and professional. Lincoln quickly checked his pockets, knowing he had no documents with him. "I don't have it here. I left it at home. I'll bring it later," he said, trying to sound casual, though impatience slipped into his voice. Ju-Yin nodded slightly, her pulse quickening. She smoothly pressed a hidden alert button under the desk while keeping her expression impassive, projecting only mild inconvenience at his missing ID.

"Without a physical ID, I can't proceed with your request," she said, her voice calm, as Lincoln's frustration became apparent. He leaned forward, placing his hands on Ju-Yin's desk. "Lincoln Sorní, look me up in the system," he ordered, brusquely reaching toward her computer.

Ju-Yin's jaw tightened almost imperceptibly as she withdrew her hands. "Mr. Sorní, without an ID, I can't proceed. It's for your own security," she reiterated gently, but her attempt to calm him only seemed to fuel his anger.

"What security? I'm right here! Don't you see me?" he snapped, his voice rising, drawing the attention of nearby clients.

Ju-Yin's expression remained placid, her jaw set as she watched his outburst unfold.

"You know what, you're inept. I don't want my money here anymore. I want all my money in cash right now!" He paused, hearing himself, then nodded. "Yes, give me all my money now."

Ju-Yin's face didn't falter, but her jaw tensed. Not even her mother or father would have dared to speak to her that way. She took a deep breath, knowing that an inappropriate reaction could jeopardize her career. Just then, the security guard, a robust man with an imposing presence, approached with firm steps, his eyes taking in the tension in the room. Without showing irritation, Ju-Yin glanced toward the approaching guard, catching his eye before returning her attention to Lincoln.

"Is there a problem here, sir?" the guard asked, his deep, controlled voice resonating in the tense air. His gaze shifted briefly to Ju-Yin, acknowledging her calm control before focusing back on Lincoln.

"Yes, I don't want my money here anymore, and this *idiot* won't transfer my money," Lincoln replied, pointing at Ju-Yin with frustration.

The guard's eyes narrowed slightly at Lincoln's outburst, but his expression remained impassive. He stepped closer to Lincoln, his presence radiating an unshakable authority.

"Sir, I ask that you maintain respect," the guard said in a firm tone, keeping his calm. "The staff is here to assist you, but we need your cooperation."

"Security, please escort this man out of my office," Ju-Yin ordered, her voice firm but with an undertone of offense.

"Escort me out of here?" Lincoln exclaimed, offended, his face flushed with indignation. "Customers like me put food on your table!"

"Security, please call the authorities..." Ju-Yin said firmly.

"I'm the one who's going to call the police because my rights are being violated here!" Lincoln shouted, becoming more agitated.

The guard approached him, and grabbed him.

"Let go of me! I'm a distinguished customer here!" He tried to break free, but the guard's strength kept him firmly under control.

The guard dragged him toward the exit, causing a commotion that made everyone in the bank turn to look.

"Transfer my money, bitch!" Lincoln shouted, completely losing control. "Transfer my money, bitch!"

That day, Lincoln was handcuffed and escorted to the police station by two officers, both of Mexican descent. The coincidence created a bond of empathy between them and Lincoln. At the station, after Lincoln recounted the tragedy of losing his wife and child, it was determined that he did not pose a threat to society. However, due to his behavior being altered by substance abuse, it was decided to keep him in a controlled environment to prevent him from sabotaging himself.

At midnight, when Lincoln finally felt like himself again, one of the officers drove him back to his home in SoHo. Throughout the entire journey, Lincoln didn't say a word. He kept his gaze fixed on whatever was beyond the window, while one or two tears slid down his cheeks. He knew Kenny's fate after being left alone, neglected, and drugged. The car's motion felt endless, dragging him toward a reality he was unwilling to face

"Is there anyone waiting for you at home, sir?" the officer asked.

Lincoln took longer than necessary to respond.When he thought he was ready, his tongue betrayed him, and only his head moved side to side, shaking in denial and sentencing himself to the longest walk of his short life. He knew his son was dead from the moment he came out of his delirium. He couldn't stop crying, and although the officers thought he was mourning the tragedy of his son and wife in the ocean, Lincoln was weeping for the murder of his own child, a secret he vowed to keep until the day of his own death.

At 2:45 a.m., Lincoln found himself standing in front of the main door. As he approached the door to listen inside, all he could recognize was the wild pounding of his own heart. Paying closer attention to the noises within, he heard only emptiness, the silence that comes when there's nothing. And there, in that nothingness, he couldn't help but wonder: What would he do with his newborn's body after tiring of holding him, kissing him, and asking for his forgiveness? What would he do when his tiny body began to smell of death, when his skin turned cold as ice and took on the purple hue of the dead? No question found an answer, but he did find the strength to open the door and enter. Inside, the air was heavy with foul odors: they could have been coming from the trash piled up under the sink, which Santiago used to take care of every day, or perhaps it was the staleness; the windows hadn't been opened in a long time. It might also have been the smell of sweat; the sheets hadn't been washed for ages. Or maybe it was the scent of dirty laundry, of underwear stained and crusted with dried semen. It could also have been the smell of used towels from the bathroom, thrown into the laundry basket, where, instead of drying, they had grown bacteria due to the moisture. When Lincoln entered the room, the stench of excrement hit his nose in a nauseating way. As he walked in, his eyes were already fixed on the crib, and the first thing he saw was Kenny, awake, staring at the ceiling, serious and thoughtful, as if lost in deep reflections. Lincoln picked him up and hugged him with desperation, regardless of the odor of shit, then pulled him away because the stench was stronger than his private sorrow.

On another sleepless night, Lincoln sat amidst the remnants of his non very productive day and the memories of his deceased wife. He donned her wedding dress and, as tears streamed down his cheeks, applied makeup, improvising an enthusiastic expression. With the music's volume climbing, Lincoln, in a flight of ecstasy,

155

rose like a puppet brought to life, dancing around the room, the long dress swaying to the melody. Kenny, still crying and with an empty stomach, couldn't help but be intrigued by the ambiguous, shameless figure dancing so intensely. However, his introspection was interrupted by the doorbell.

Outside, a man with an athletic build and strong features waited, bearing a striking resemblance—whether by coincidence or not—to the nearly forgotten face of Derrick. Lincoln wasn't surprised by his presence, but he scrutinized him closely. The stranger let out a laugh at the sight of Lincoln distorted in that wedding dress.

"I'm sorry!" he apologized, lowering his head and covering his mouth to stifle further laughter.

Lincoln didn't care; his being was now nothing more than flesh, bones, drugs, and a shameless energy.

"What's your name?" Lincoln asked firmly.

"Derek."

"Derrick!" He corrected.

"Derrick," the man repeated, this time with more confidence, as if claiming the name he had been given.

"What's your name?" Lincoln insisted.

"Derrick," the man answered with firmness now.

Lincoln didn't believe him, but having him there, he left the door open and retreated to his room.

The man's real name was Charlie. Upon entering the loft, Charlie silently criticized the audacity of seeing a luxury space reduced to disorder and filth. It was a crime, he thought. He wondered how someone as young and disturbed as Lincoln could live in a place like this. In the living room, he found Kenny lying in the crib. Upon seeing him, Kenny began to cry. Charlie picked him up and tried to soothe him, but the crying didn't stop. Noticing that Lincoln had locked himself in the bathroom, Charlie took Kenny to the kitchen. Opening the fridge, he found nothing suitable to feed the child. The cupboards were equally empty. Although he had noticed a bottle with oat water on the counter, he hesitated to give it to the child, as it looked like it had been sitting there for hours. However, with no other option, he offered the bottle to Kenny, who, hungry or thirsty, drank its entire contents, including the twelve drops of GBL that Lincoln, out of pure fear, had decided to pour in but *not* to give him.

When Lincoln came out of the bathroom, he was wearing loose gray joggers tied at the hips, which revealed his slender body and the two long lines on his lower abs. He would have said that he was ripped, but it was merely a result of caloric deficit. His face, though clearly given some attention, still bore the remnants of poorly applied makeup. As he stepped out, he noticed Kenny latched onto the bottle, eagerly drinking the oat water. Lincoln, visibly irritated, abruptly yanked it out of his mouth, confusing Charlie.

"Is it expired?" Charlie asked, clueless about the situation.

Kenny began to cry loudly, and Lincoln, after a moment of thought, put the bottle back in his mouth.

"I couldn't find anything else, so..." Charlie began to explain.

Lincoln interrupted him as he walked toward the bedroom: "Put him in the crib, take off your clothes, and follow me," he said confidently.

Charlie, at his age, had already had many wealthy clients, and in all of them, he found one common trait: confidence. He quickly sensed it in Lincoln, not knowing the reality behind it, because the truth was that Lincoln wasn't confident; he simply didn't care about anything or anyone anymore. He no longer felt the need to impress others; he just wanted to feel sexually satisfied, to the point of exhaustion, so he could fall asleep like a stone. If he didn't wake up from sleep, he would consider himself fortunate. But that was his problem: he never felt completely satisfied with sex, and the methamphetamine prevented him from sleeping.

When Charlie entered the bedroom, Lincoln was sitting on the edge of the bed, smoking crystal meth from a glass pipe.

"Sit down," Lincoln ordered, indicating a spot beside him.

Charlie sat down. Lincoln brought the pipe closer to his mouth.

"Is it necessary?" Charlie asked, uncomfortable.

Lincoln studied him for a moment, then nodded.

Charlie smoked because it had been agreed upon when Lincoln contacted him through the *red* website, but also because he thought that by pleasing Lincoln, many doors could open for him in the future. It was impossible not to think that Lincoln was as wealthy as he seemed, and given the obvious circumstances, Lincoln was more alone and lost than a needle in a haystack. Considering his physical and intellectual advantages over Lincoln, Charlie decided to do whatever was necessary to please him. With other clients, Charlie would usually *fake* smoking, but with Lincoln, he made the biggest exception of his life, risking it all because he knew that meth addiction was a dangerous game. Lincoln stared at him, unblinking, until he found just the right angle of light that made Charlie look eerily like Derrick. When he finally saw it, Lincoln's mind was already clouded by the *substance*.

"Derrick?" Lincoln asked, dazed, blurring the line between reality and hallucination.

"Lincoln?" Charlie replied.

"Where did you go?" Lincoln's voice trembled with tears, a deep worry etched in his tone.

"I'm right here, baby."

"Baby?" Lincoln asked, disgusted. "Derrick would never call me 'baby,'" he said, irritated.

"Boy!" Charlie said instinctively.

"Is it you?" Lincoln asked, melancholic, grabbing Charlie's chin, but upon seeing his eyes, he shook his head. "No, you're not Derrick."

"I am Derrick," Charlie insisted, his voice steady.

"No, you're not Derrick," Lincoln said. "You're weak."

"Who's weak?" Charlie shot back, gripping Lincoln's throat with unexpected force.

"Derrick, is that you?" Lincoln whispered, caught between fear and desire, clutching the hand tightening around his neck.

Charlie, noticing how Lincoln responded to the pressure, began to understand the personality of Derrick. What started as a simple game turned into a deep dive into Derrick's character, with each of Lincoln's reactions painting a clearer picture. Derrick had been a man of strength, and as Charlie explored this role, every movement drew a precise response from Lincoln, blurring the lines between pain and pleasure.

Hours passed in their role-playing, and both became so absorbed in the dynamic that they completely forgot about Kenny, who, malnourished and under the influence of the 12 drops of GBL, slept deeply.

Outside, the day had already dawned, but inside the loft, darkness reigned. Sixteen hours had passed since Charlie's arrival. Both were still under the influence of the substances, but Lincoln began to feel drowsy, a side effect of the GBL that Charlie had intentionally overdosed in his drink to finally make him sleep. Lincoln had seemed unstoppable until now.

"What do you do for work? How come you have so much money?" Charlie asked, his curiosity mingled with a calculated interest. He wasn't just making small talk; he was probing for a deeper understanding of Lincoln's financial situation, weighing the possibilities of how he could benefit from it.

"I am a writer."

"Are you famous? " Charlie asked, curious about Lincoln's influence.

"Have you read my work?" Lincoln asked, his voice wavering.

"No, but I could," Charlie replied, a mix of curiosity and a growing desire to please. He knew that winning Lincoln's favor could open doors, not just emotionally, but financially.

"I doubt you can read."

"I can read... not much, but I read some things," Charlie said, shameless. "Who is Derrick?" he asked, eager to understand more about the man he was playing the part.

"My husband," Lincoln lied, but something in him believed it was true.

"Where is he?" Charlie asked, now with genuine interest, considering the possibilities that would arise if Derrick didn't return.

"I don't know. He left," Lincoln admitted, his voice barely a whisper. "But he'll come back," he added, with a determination that Charlie found almost naive.

"How do you know he'll come back?"

"Because I'll wait for him."

Charlie found the reason stupid.

"That doesn't guarantee he'll return."

Lincoln looked at him, his eyes shining with a pain that Charlie couldn't, or perhaps didn't want to, fully comprehend. But then Lincoln said something that made Charlie's mind race.

"One day he'll come back for his son."

"Oh, that's his son?" Charlie tried to hide his surprise, but his mind was already calculating.

"He's our son... what if he never comes back?" Charlie asked, planting the seed of doubt with the subtlety of a seasoned manipulator.

Lincoln opened his eyes to watch him, his eyes now more focused, as if awakening from a dream.

"If he never comes back... then you can stay," Lincoln said, after selling Charlie on the idea of his false abundance.

Charlie smiled, openly, after noticing that lincoln gave up consciousness.

Lincoln drifted into a deep sleep that lasted approximately 18 hours. It was so deep that there were no nightmares, no dreams—just a black, silent void.

The smell of *Fabuloso* cleaner woke him. Opening his eyes, he was met with a sharp pain in his neck from an awkward position on the pillow. The room was clean and organized, reminiscent of the days when Jo Lynn was still alive. When he stood up, his feet ached from the long hours of inactivity, but after a moment, he steadied himself and walked to the living room, where everything was immaculate, in its place. Soup was simmering on the stove, and lasagna was browning in the oven. Across the room, by the window overlooking the street, Charlie sat with Kenny in his arms, feeding him from a bottle.

Lincoln opened the refrigerator, finding it full, then checked the pantry—it was stocked.

"Look who's finally awake ," Charlie joked, showing Kenny the worn-out remnants of his father. But the positive energy quickly faded as Lincoln's dissatisfied expression darkened the room.

"What are you still doing here?" Lincoln asked, irritation clear in his voice.

Charlie visibly flinched, feeling insulted after everything he had done for Lincoln while he slept.

"Your son was crying, there was no food, so I went out and bought some. I thought you'd wake up hungry.

"Don't take liberties that aren't yours. No one asked you to do any of that."

Charlie was left speechless, unsure where to channel his next move.

"I'm sorry, that wasn't my intention," he said, apologetic. "Do you like lasagna? My mother taught me, and she says mine is even better than hers now."

"Maybe you should go see your mother," Lincoln replied, dripping with sarcasm.

"My mother doesn't live here." Charlie responded, his voice tinged with sadness, missing her.

"Don't you have a home?" Lincoln asked, his intention clear to offend.

"I do, but I wasn't sure if my service was over."

"Your service ended a long time ago."

Charlie looked at him, disappointment flooding his veins, but then anger overtook it, spreading through him like poison.

"Cash or Venmo?" he asked, his voice tight.

"Venmo," Lincoln answered, casually popping two Tylenols.

Charlie pulled out his phone and calculated the total.

"Your total is 25.6 thousand dollars."

"You're crazy!" Lincoln scoffed.

"64 hours at 400 dollars an hour is 25.6 thousand." Charlie explained, double-checking the math on his phone.

Lincoln burst into laughter at Charlie's naivety.

"I don't know what world you live in, but in mine, no one pays 25 grand to a prostitute."

"You can pay with Venmo or cash." Charlie repeated, his voice trembling, fear creeping in at the thought of what he might do if Lincoln continued to refuse.

"I can give you 1,200 at most." Lincoln confirmed, sounding satisfied.

"64 hours at 400 an hour is 25.6 thousand, not 1,200. You owe me 25.6 thousand dollars. Are you going to pay in cash or Venmo?" Charlie repeated to himself, staring at the floor, his anger barely contained.

If Lincoln had taken the time to get to know Charlie, he would have discovered that he had spent more than twelve years in juvenile prison after his twin brother confessed that they had both drowned their newborn baby brother in the bathtub. If Lincoln had made the effort to know him better, he would have understood that Charlie had a clinical history of depression, anxiety, and anger that he could only control with medication. If Lincoln had dug deeper, he would have known that the U.S. government had given Charlie his name to protect his identity after his release. And if Lincoln had understood Charlie's near-total illiteracy, he would have realized that his work as an escort was his only source of income. If Lincoln had seen Charlie for what he really was—a young man trapped in his own hell—he would never have risked his life over a debt.

Charlie left the loft with a set of *Louis Vuitton* luggage, filled with Jo Lynn's high-end shoes, jewelry, bags, and dresses, which he later sold for a sum exceeding 100,000 dollars. Unaware of the quality of those items, he couldn't help but be surprised by the amount of money he got for them, and with little remorse, but with the fear of being caught by the authorities, he ventured to leave New York and move to Miami, where he could escape the law, but not karma.

Before leaving the loft, in a fit of rage and frustration, Charlie had knocked Lincoln to the ground with a blow, leaving him injured. Then, he unleashed his fury by kicking him all over his body, unknowingly breaking a rib, which made it impossible for Lincoln to breathe normally. Lincoln lay there on the ground like a dying dog, unable to move. Each breath was a torment, as if with each one his soul was being torn out, while Kenny cried from hunger, with his father, who wasn't really his father, unable to get up to feed him. It would have taken Lincoln two hours and twenty-five minutes to get up off the floor, but the lasagna burning in the oven, the soup evaporating, and the smell of Kenny's feces didn't allow him to stay down. With difficulty, he crawled to the oven to turn it off, then stood up to turn off the stove, changed Kenny's diapers, took three *Tylenol*, and got into the bathtub with warm water, hoping to soothe the sharp pain in his rib, which, unbeknownst to him, was broken. Soon he felt frustrated, as neither the Tylenol nor the warm water managed to relieve his pain. When the pain became even more unbearable, he remembered Derrick, when he said that *Ketamine* is the medicine for pain. After consuming it, he felt immediate relief that not only allowed him to move more freely but also awakened a voracious appetite, leading him to devour the burnt lasagna without complaint. At bedtime, the bed felt as hard as a rock. Unable to find a comfortable spot, he turned again to *ketamine* and GBL, falling asleep almost immediately. But for the first time, he woke up in the middle of the night, just two hours later, and couldn't get back to sleep, so he consumed more GBL and slept for another two hours. This pattern repeated itself over and over, and in doing so, he discovered a cycle that fed his new addiction.

In the days following the assault, Lincoln focused on managing the pain from his broken rib and bruises with *ketamine*, while also applying cold compresses to the bruise that was beginning to spread. He refused to go to the hospital. Lincoln had always been very healthy; the last time he visited a hospital was in his native Mexico, where you have to wait all day in a room full of sick people, only to finally be seen by a doctor who prescribes ibuprofen twice a day and tells you to rest and drink plenty of fluids. Lincoln was already following that advice, finding the pending visit to the doctor unnecessary—he felt that practical and smart.

Five days after the assault, Lincoln decided to pay a visit. When he arrived, he recognized Santiago, dressed in his Spider-Man costume. Lincoln approached Santiago and donated $100 to his cause. Santiago was taken aback when he saw him; their eyes met, pausing as they tried to decipher the appropriate emotion to express in this unexpected encounter. Lincoln smiled nervously. Santiago responded with a warm smile before hugging him, and Lincoln couldn't help but cry as he returned the embrace.

"Everything's going to be okay," Santiago whispered.

Lincoln said nothing, but nodded, burying his face in Santiago's neck. Santiago gently pulled away, worried about what people on the street might think of their display of affection.

He turned to Kenny's stroller, opened the plastic cover, and noticed that the child was still asleep. He lifted him into his arms, and the light weight of his body immediately revealed his malnutrition. Despite the noise of *Times Square* and being handled by Santiago, Kenny didn't react, which immediately aroused Santiago's suspicion. Lincoln saw the concern and discontent on Santiago's face, and before he could judge him and bombard him with questions, he took Kenny and placed him back in the stroller.

"If you wake him, he won't stop crying, and you'll be the one to take him home crying," Lincoln said, his tone irritated and his gaze severe, trying to disguise his nervousness. This reaction only deepened Santiago's suspicion.

"Get out of here. I'll see you later at your place," Santiago said, not waiting for an invitation.

Lincoln smiled and nodded, accepting the self-invitation. He wanted to hug him to close the encounter, but Santiago, sensing the energy and silent intention, abruptly returned to his Spider-Man duties. Lincoln, satisfied that the differences between him and Santiago were now in the past, left. After Lincoln's departure, Santiago didn't earn another dollar. Watching him leave, he couldn't help but worry about Lincoln's mental health and Kenny's well-being, as it was evident that both were lacking proper care. Torn by his concern, he debated whether to forget about them and continue with his simple life or to act like a true superhero and intervene, knowing that *crystal meth*, as cursed as it is, was a major part of the problem. Later, Santiago stood in front of Lincoln's door for about ten minutes. His fear wasn't entering that apartment, but the possibility of never being able to leave, trapped in a whirlwind of emotions that he didn't want to get involved in, much less commit to. He didn't just fear the consequences of the drugs Lincoln consumed, but also the person he became under their influence. That sexual, bestial, and homosexual creature confused him; as much as he desired it, it terrified him, and he only knew one way to face it. Suddenly, the door opened, and Lincoln found Santiago there, mute and brooding.When Santiago entered the apartment, the air was thick with the smell of smoke that lingered and collided with the walls. The space, once orderly and immaculate, now felt claustrophobic, with shadows clinging to the corners as if they had a life of their own. The furniture was disheveled, cushions scattered haphazardly, and clothes strewn across the floor as if they had been hastily abandoned. The windows were covered with heavy curtains, blocking out the light and leaving the room in a perpetual, suffocating twilight. Empty bottles and dirty dishes were piled up on every surface and in the sink. Everything in the apartment seemed to suffer from chronic neglect and a desperation that died in silence. It was a place where time stood still, where it was always night. Santiago, determined to break the oppressive atmosphere, pulled back the curtains and opened the windows, letting in the light and the cold night air.

"What are you doing, Santiago?" Lincoln asked, visibly irritated, frowning at the sudden invasion of light and cold.

"You can't live like this," Santiago replied, his tone a mix of frustration and concern.

"This is how we *like* to live," Lincoln retorted angrily, yanking the curtains shut, trying to restore the stifling darkness he had grown accustomed to.

Santiago, even more irritated, reopened them firmly, his patience wearing thin. Lincoln, wasting no time, tried to close them again, but the weariness in his eyes betrayed his stubbornness.

"Close the curtains when I'm gone, please," Santiago implored, his voice trembling with a desperate plea, hoping Lincoln would see what he saw.

Lincoln didn't respond.

Santiago turned to Kenny, his concern evident in every movement, and examined him carefully.

"Kenny isn't eating well," he said, his voice filled with anxiety as he looked at the child's pale, thin face.

"He's eating better than I am," Lincoln replied bitterly, though his tone hinted at a resignation that suggested he knew Santiago was right.

"How much do you weigh?" Santiago pressed, his voice a blend of sternness and worry as he observed Lincoln's underweight, emaciated frame.

"I need to get back to the gym," Lincoln said, evading the question, his voice a faint whisper of the energy he once had.

"Have you eaten?" Santiago asked.

"We had pizza."

"Kenny eats pizza now too?" Santiago asked sarcastically, his gaze fixed on the blender in the kitchen, where a red sauce suggested Lincoln might have blended the pizza to feed Kenny.

"Kenny has a good appetite," Lincoln replied cynically.

Santiago took a deep breath, controlling his anger to avoid a scene. He went to the kitchen and began preparing Kenny's food, noticing that the cans of formula were unopened.

Santiago was a blessed soul, and besides his mother, only God knew it. That night, when Lincoln asked if he wanted to stay, he replied:

"I have a *client*," he lied, trying to manipulate Lincoln's loneliness. Winter had brought many expenses and little income, and although he desperately needed the money to cover his family's holiday obligations, he also suspected that Lincoln, after Jo Lynn's death, must have been amassing a substantial fortune.

Lincoln offered to pay him the amount the supposed client was offering if he stayed. Santiago played hard to get but finally agreed, on the condition that Lincoln wouldn't use *methamphetamine*.

"I don't touch that crap anymore," Lincoln replied, lying to himself.

Although Santiago didn't believe him, he decided not to contradict him, knowing it could drive him away from his true goal: indulging in recreational drugs and losing himself in *romance* and pleasure in Lincoln's arms.

Santiago had an active sex life with his girlfriend, Natalie, but he only felt fully satisfied when he fantasized about the presence of a male figure. That's why, in their sexual encounters, he relied on pornography featuring white women and well-endowed men. Although Natalie found the pornography increasingly strange and unnecessary, she never challenged it because she had been taught that men were the most complex and incomplete beings on the planet. For his part, Santiago didn't dare mention the possibility of male participation in their intimacy, as he was too reserved and she, too insecure. Thus, Lincoln became his only gateway to ecstasy and the exile of his own lies. What he enjoyed most about those drugs was how they stripped him of his inhibitions, transforming him into a man free of taboos and fears, a man who carried his deepest desires with pride—the very desires that, in the light of day, would be his most diabolical sins. When no one was watching, when no one could read his thoughts, and when his father's machismo-laden words faded from his mind, Santiago longed to be like that always, without needing those damned drugs. And while he waited for that day that might never come, Santiago found himself locked in the bathroom, secretly dosing himself with *ketamine* and GBL. Fearing that Lincoln might notice his euphoria, he nibbled on the euphorix, consuming only a fifth of the pill. When Santiago emerged from the bathroom, Lincoln was getting into bed for the first time, determined to sleep or at least rest, because his broken rib hurt like an exorcised demon. Ever since Santiago had arrived, and out of respect for him, Lincoln had refrained from using *ketamine* or any other drug that would turn him into an animal—one that, after showing its savagery, is negligently abandoned to the mercy of solitude.

"What are you doing?" Santiago asked, annoyed, suspecting that Lincoln just wanted to lie down and sleep like a dog.

Lincoln tried to respond, but the pain from his broken rib barely let him breathe.

"What's wrong?" Santiago insisted, noticing Lincoln's evident discomfort. He could hear it in Lincoln's soft groans and see it in his careful movements. But despite the pain, Lincoln remained silent, wearing an oversized NIRVANA t-shirt.

"Nothing, I'm just tired," Lincoln replied.

Santiago undressed and got into bed. He rested his head on his hand and watched Lincoln, who lay beside him staring at the ceiling, one hand protecting his broken rib. Frustration and desire built up in Santiago, feeling ignored by Lincoln's indifference. Lincoln, for his part, had already noticed the lightness in Santiago's eyes, a product of the *euphorix*, and the sexual intentions that drove him. He let out a laugh, seeing the irony of the situation—now it was Santiago, the one on drugs, wanting sex.

"What?" Santiago snapped, feeling exposed and judged.

"What do you want?" Lincoln asked, making it clear he wasn't about to give in.

Santiago watched him in silence for a moment before asking him to take off his t-shirt. Lincoln, aware of his bruises and what that would reveal, firmly refused. He didn't want to expose his bruises, and for the first time, he didn't feel like having sex; he just wanted to rest on his back to ease the pain and sleep deeply, like a baby. Santiago, under the influence of the drugs, let his fingers trace Lincoln's arm, the touch heavy with a boldness he wouldn't otherwise allow himself, but also simmering with resentment at Lincoln's newfound detachment. If Santiago hadn't taken the drugs he had, he never would've dared to touch Lincoln between his legs. And if Lincoln had taken the drugs he hadn't, he wouldn't have had the audacity to reject him. The night before, Lincoln had promised himself not to take drugs again. It wasn't the first time he'd made that promise, and even though he had sworn to himself countless times, he always ended up falling back, cloaked in shame. But Lincoln still believed—almost blindly—that if he tried hard enough, one day he'd stop falling. And that night, he felt like that moment had finally come. *Ketamine* eased the physical pain, but each dose sickened his soul, sinking him deeper into the darkness that had trapped him for so long. Each time he took it, he craved other substances, and the real problem wasn't just succumbing to them—it was that once he started, he couldn't stop. It was an endless cycle, a downward spiral that suffocated him slowly. And although it temporarily relieved his body, it destroyed him inside, leaving scars much deeper than the physical ones.

"What are you doing?" Lincoln asked, holding his gaze, trying to shame him, but his attempt was in vain.

Santiago, under the influence of the drugs, felt a twisted satisfaction in Lincoln's vulnerability, though it was tainted by a simmering anger at Lincoln's detachment. "I want you to fuck me," Santiago said, direct and without hesitation. That night, Lincoln wrestled with a complex depression, the result of excessive *methamphetamine* and other drugs. He felt cruel for having drugged his son out of convenience and like an addict losing control over his life.

"I'm not going to pay you," Lincoln said firmly, trying to kill Santiago's passion.

"Who's asking for money?" Santiago shot back, blending offense with defiance.

"And your girlfriend?" Lincoln asked, confronting Santiago with his own fears, searching for a response that might force Santiago to face reality.

"Are you going to let me fuck you or *not*?" Santiago replied, his tone shifting to aggression, driven by both desire and desperation.

Lincoln didn't answer, instead studying Santiago's behavior closely. Santiago leaned in, bringing his mouth close to Lincoln's as though Lincoln were an object of desire. So close that Lincoln could taste the salt on his skin; Santiago hadn't showered.

"So what are you going to do?" he asked, his tone laced with intimidation.

"So, you are gay after all," Lincoln said, as if he had just discovered the obvious.

"Would you let me fuck you if I said I was?" Santiago replied, possessed by a defiant force he didn't recognize. It was a wild, masculine blend that suited his virile attributes.

Lincoln smiled, satisfied to confirm what he already suspected. And although he could have pleased him, he pushed him away, because his exhaustion was greater than the desire to entertain him. For a moment, Santiago hesitated, caught off guard by Lincoln's visible rejection, but then his frustration broke through. He leaned closer, trying one last time to bridge the widening chasm between them. But Lincoln took a deliberate step back, his face closed off, a wall now firmly in place.

"Don't make this harder than it has to be, Santiago," he added, his voice softened, but the message as sharp as ever.

"You're *the* homosexual!" Santiago exclaimed, pushing Lincoln's arm away with offended force. As he did, Lincoln's rib erupted in sharp pain, forcing him to steady his breath and stifle the instinct to scream, masking his agony behind a tight-lipped expression.

"I'm *no* homosexual," Lincoln replied, clutching his rib. The final push felt dangerous. Lincoln knew Santiago could take it as a permanent end, but he wasn't ready for that—not completely. The thought of being alone gnawed at him, so he softened, unwilling to provoke Santiago too much.

"You write love poems to men," Santiago accused him. *"Derrick, I can't live without you. Derrick, please come back."* He mimicked him dramatically.

Despite the pain, Lincoln was in shock.

"Derrick is a fictional character," he clarified. "Since when have you been reading my stuff?"

"Well, isn't that why you write?"

"Not for you to read!" Lincoln retorted, offended.

"You're obsessed with that Derrick."

Lincoln shot back sarcastically, "You're the one begging me to let you fuck me."

"Wait a minute," Santiago said, analyzing the situation. "That Derrick... is me. I'm the Derrick in your diaries."

Speechless, Lincoln stared at him, admiring his sudden creativity in solving mysteries.

"Am I?" Santiago asked, incredulous.

Lincoln didn't answer, but he watched him carefully. Santiago stood still, processing what he had just uncovered. The narrative he had imagined for himself began to unravel, and a confusion of feelings—desire, guilt, fear—overwhelmed him. He didn't know how to fit into the story that Lincoln seemed to have written for them both. He asked himself with doubt and guilt, "But I didn't hurt you, did I?" Then, turning to Lincoln, Santiago added, "You love me. You really love me," his voice soft, as if confessing to himself, while revisiting in his mind the diaries he had read. Lincoln observed him in silence. Santiago muttered, hurt, "I don't know if I love you like that." Lincoln recognized Santiago's vulnerability and confusion in those words and, without thinking, moved closer.

"You know it, but you're scared."

"I'm not like you."

"Maybe you're not like me, and maybe I'm not like you. But if we feel the same, it must be because we are the same," Lincoln said, intending to confuse him.

"No, I have a girlfriend."

"And I'm a widower, with a son."

"My parents would kill me."

"They won't kill you. They'll kick you out."

Santiago couldn't help but feel scared.

"And if they kick you out, you can move here. You love Kenny, and he loves you. Together, we can do so much," Lincoln promised with excitement.

Most people dream of living in New York, but New York City is so vast that it's impossible not to feel alone. And once you can't leave, you end up surviving your own loneliness. Although Lincoln wasn't born in New York, he would probably die there, and while waiting for that day to come, he saw in Santiago the opportunity to feel less alone.

"Can we have sex and talk about this another day?" Santiago asked, feeling overwhelmed and chaotic.

Lincoln smiled, nodded, and gave in to the ketamine and GBL to calm his pain. Under the influence of the drugs, Lincoln and Santiago attempted to make love, but every movement, even with the numbing effects of the ketamine, sent sharp, unbearable pain through Lincoln's ribs. Santiago, frustrated by the interruption, tried to press on, but Lincoln's discomfort forced them both to stop. Santiago insisted that Lincoln take off his Nirvana shirt, and when he saw the bruise in the shape of a map, his concern was immediate. Before Santiago could say anything, Lincoln cut him off: "The doctor already saw it. Said it always gets worse before it gets better." Lincoln was lying, but only partly. He hadn't seen a doctor, but he was convinced things always got worse before they got better. Santiago half-believed him, trusting that Lincoln had seen a doctor, though the idea didn't sit right with him. After thinking it over, he let it go but made Lincoln promise to visit the doctor again the next day. Santiago wanted to go with him, but he had already committed to taking his mother shopping for Christmas Eve, which was just *three days* away. At five in the morning, Santiago stood up, got dressed, and hurried toward the train, desperate to get home before his mother realized his absence and started asking questions. But before he left, Lincoln, fearful, asked, "Did you like my writing?"

Santiago sat down beside him, and for the first time in a long while, recognized in Lincoln's gaze the naive young man who once dressed up as Spider-Man with broken shoes because he couldn't afford new ones.

"I don't know who invented words," Santiago began, "but it had to be someone like you."

Lincoln wanted to cry but instead smiled.

"I want you to come to my family's Christmas Eve dinner."

"No!" Lincoln replied quickly, knowing Santiago was asking out of courtesy. Even though Santiago had never mentioned it outright, Lincoln had a feeling Santiago wasn't keen on introducing him to his family. Alone on the bed, he was left with his thoughts. Driven by a doomed idea, Lincoln grabbed one of his journals from the broken drawer of the nightstand and wrote:

```
In every sense, he was not a simple
man, and how could he be?
```

So complex was that man that his
true name, confused, slipped away
from him. And the name he invented
to replace it, insecure, never
reached him. In that sense, we were
both destined to lose ourselves
and to find each other, almost, at
the same time.

During the three days following Santiago's
departure, Lincoln only left the dining table
to prepare his and Kenny's meals, bathe him,
change his diapers, rock him, and take him out
for a walk in his stroller. On those walks, he
sought inspiration in memories that, though
recent, were already getting lost in the confusion
of events clouded by the effects of drugs. But
in the long, hot showers, he pieced together
fragments that came to life. Still dripping wet,
he would rush back to the dining room and, in
front of the window that now bathed the once-
darkened space in light, would write quickly
on his computer, afraid that those fragments,
heavy with their toxic fragility, might crumble
and be lost from his memory forever. On the
third day, without having finished it—because
his nights fell before the day ended—he titled
it simply: *The Man I Adored.* Throughout
that third day, Santiago sent Lincoln insistent
messages, confirming his presence at the
Christmas Eve dinner in Astoria. Immersed in
the frantic writing of his story, Lincoln ignored

the messages. By the end of the day, driven by the desperation of loneliness— which always wears the face of a slaughtered dog— he decided to attend the dinner only because Santiago had extended an invitation to a circuit party that would take place later that same Christmas Eve. Lincoln, who had stopped going to such parties during his relationship with Jo Lynn, now preferred to seek out men online, invite them over, and indulge in long sessions of pornography and sex under the influence of drugs' sweet nectar. The idea of diving back into that ocean of pretentious muscle-bound men, only to be judged cruelly, didn't appeal to him. But his firm intention to give in to one last night of excess, a symbolic closing of those damned days that gave him so little and ended up taking everything, provided the motivation to go. After that night, he promised himself he would dedicate what remained of his life to picking up the broken pieces of his existence—and then, those of his poor son. At six in the evening, Lincoln took his tenth shower of the day. He then dressed in a long black *Ferragamo* coat that fell to his knees; inside, he felt warm, while outside, the cold was brutal. By seven, he faced the dilemma of finding a babysitter for Kenny, but being Christmas Eve, it was impossible to find anyone available on such short notice. By eight, restless, he found himself in front of a bottle of amber—GBL—and a difficult decision to make.

Santiago and his parents, Camila and Francisco, had spent the last three days organizing the preparations for Christmas Eve dinner. Cooking the meat had taken them two full days. Despite all the meticulous planning, when it came time to set the table, everyone was running late. They hurried to finish cooking, bathe, get dressed in their new clothes, unpack the dishes, and set the table. Each of them, caught up in their own chaos, was trying to impose order amid the disorder when the doorbell rang. Santiago, excited, ran to the door. All day he had been eagerly looking forward to seeing Lincoln like never before. However, when he opened the door, he was surprised to find Natalie, his girlfriend, with her cheeks flushed from the cold and her breath visible in the chilly air. She wore a long red coat that reached down to her ankles, which she had bought that same day at Buffalo Exchange, and a wool hat from the previous winter that covered her forehead. Santiago tried to hide his disappointment upon seeing her, but his face betrayed him.

"I thought you were working tonight," Santiago said, confused, as she quickly stepped inside to escape the cold.

"I quit," she responded, satisfied, as she removed her secondhand coat. Santiago looked even more confused. Natalie leaned in to kiss him.

"Happy birthday, love," she whispered in his ear, pulling an envelope from her pocket and handing it to him.

"Natalie, dear, weren't you supposed to work today?" Camila asked as she approached.

"I took the day off," Natalie responded, smiling as she greeted her mother-in-law with a kiss on the cheek. Camila, who always enjoyed Natalie's company, welcomed her warmly, taking her by the arm and leading her into the kitchen. Santiago, on the other hand, felt a pang of frustration. His girlfriend's sudden arrival unsettled him, especially since he knew that Lincoln and Natalie didn't get along. As he closed the door, he saw Lincoln struggling to climb the stairs, clearly uncomfortable due to the pain in his ribs.

"Didn't you go to the doctor?" Santiago asked, concerned, as he moved toward him to help.

"No," Lincoln replied through gritted teeth.

"I told you to go," he scolded him.

"I was busy," Lincoln admitted.

"Busy doing what?" Santiago asked sarcastically, deducing that he had been using drugs again.

"I wrote the most beautiful story in the world," Lincoln said, grabbing Santiago's arm and looking him directly in the eyes, as if confessing the sweetest secret of all. Santiago saw the sparkle in his eyes and was happy for him. For a moment, he wanted to kiss him. But his fear of being judged was greater than the urge to sin in public.

"Derrick and Lincoln, do they end up together?" Santiago asked.

"It wouldn't be the most beautiful story in the world if they end up together."

"So they didn't end up together?"

"It's not finished," Lincoln said.

"What's it called?" he asked, curious.

"The man I adored," Lincoln replied.

Santiago looked thoughtful. "Adored?" he asked with concern. "In the past?"

"You must be the famous Lincoln!" Camila exclaimed from the doorway, smiling brightly. Behind her, Natalie watched with a mix of jealousy and discomfort that she couldn't hide. Camila's enthusiastic greeting broke the intimate moment they had been sharing. Noticing the tension on Natalie's face, Santiago let go of Lincoln on the stairs and hurried to welcome everyone inside. As everyone entered the house, they found Francisco, Santiago's father, putting on his coat as he headed outside to see what all the commotion with his wife was about.

Despite being a good man with a calm temperament, Francisco always had a grumpy look on his face. After turning sixty, he became even more interested than his wife in knowing everything that was happening around him, even if it didn't concern him. When his wife criticized him for being so nosy, he simply replied, "As the head and protector of this family, it is my duty to be aware of everything that happens inside and outside this house."

185

Lincoln's visit took Francisco by surprise. Although he had heard little about him, his son had never mentioned that Lincoln was wealthy. Francisco quickly deduced this from the Ferragamo coat he was wearing, one he had previously studied when his boss had asked him to pick up a similar piece from the store. Curious, he had checked the price, and upon trying it on, he understood why rich people would pay so much for such an exclusive garment. And like many poor people, Francisco dreamed of one day owning a coat like that.

"Dad, Mom, this is Lincoln," Santiago introduced Lincoln to the family.

"Nice to meet you, I'm Camila, Santiaguito's mother," said Camila proudly, hugging Lincoln with enthusiasm. Lincoln let out a groan he hadn't anticipated due to the pain from his broken rib.

"What's wrong?" Camila reacted, alarmed.

"Lincoln..." Santiago began.

"Nothing, ma'am, don't worry," Lincoln interrupted Santiago, preventing him from mentioning the injury and drawing attention to his condition for the rest of the night.

"Sir, nice to meet you," Lincoln said, extending his hand to Francisco. Francisco, unable to stop staring at the coat, gave Lincoln a firm handshake, and upon seeing how sophisticated he looked, couldn't resist pulling him in for a hug. Lincoln let out another groan, this time more audible. Francisco and the others became alarmed. Lincoln quickly covered the area around his ribs, struggling to catch his breath and keep a low profile. Worried, Santiago pulled Lincoln away from his father, which annoyed Natalie, although Santiago didn't notice.Then he tried to take off Lincoln's coat, but Lincoln insisted on keeping it on. Camila, with her maternal instincts kicking in, aggressively approached to remove the coat. Although Lincoln insisted on keeping it, she continued trying to take it off.

"I said no!" Lincoln exclaimed firmly.

Camila stepped back, not offended but worried.

"What's wrong with you?" she asked.

"He fell and has a bruise that hasn't been checked by a doctor," Santiago explained.

"I'll warm up some arnica leaves for you, okay?" Camila offered.

"I'm fine, ma'am, thank you very much," Lincoln replied, trying to maintain his manners.

"It won't cost you anything, and it won't hurt. We don't want anything to happen to you, especially now, after the tragedy of your wife. My deepest condolences," Camila said sincerely, placing her hand over her heart.

"Ma'!" Santiago exclaimed, embarrassed by her comment.

"What did I say wrong?" Camila retorted.

"Are you married, son?" Francisco asked, shocked by Lincoln's youthful appearance.

"Yes, and he has a newborn son," Camila responded.

Francisco became even more interested in Lincoln. He hadn't expected a man with a boyish face to already be married with a child.

"What happened to your wife?" Francisco asked, curious.

"She died," Camila abruptly responded, trying to cut off her husband's insensitivity out of respect for Lincoln.

"She's dead?" he pressed.

"Yes, Francisco, she drowned," Camila confirmed with little patience.

Francisco couldn't understand how an adult could not know how to swim. How could she have drowned when all one has to do in such an emergency is float on their back?

"Didn't she know how to swim?" Francisco asked, implying that swimming was a basic skill.

"She knew how to swim, but she wanted to drown, and she did," Lincoln confessed, with a seriousness that made Francisco's hair stand on end, leaving the room in dead silence.

"Why would a married woman with a child want to drown herself?"

"Dad!" Santiago exclaimed, mortified.

"Because she found me in bed with another man," Lincoln replied, observing Francisco's reaction. For a moment, Francisco looked confused.

The revelation was a shock for everyone, including Santiago.

"What are you talking about?" Santiago asked, confused.

"Didn't you know, Santiago?" Natalie asked sarcastically from the corner, clearly angry.

Francisco and Camila caught the double meaning in Natalie's words.

Santiago glared at Natalie, angry, but his eyes betrayed his nerves, feeling exposed.

"Didn't you know your friend is obviously gay and in love with you?"

"Natalie, don't talk about things you don't know."

Suddenly, a blow was heard, and Camila's scream filled the air. When Santiago turned, he saw Lincoln on the ground with his father kicking him in the torso with the force of an animal. Santiago immediately intervened, pulling his aggressive father away from Lincoln.

"Don't touch me," Francisco, disgusted, pushed his son's hands off him.

Camila, worried, knelt beside Lincoln, who was struggling to catch the breath that the blows had knockedout of him. Camila and Santiago helped Lincoln up from the ground, and as he regained his breath, he let out a desperate cry of pain.

"Get this faggot out of my house," Francisco ordered, before retreating to his room.

"Santi, take him home," Camila requested.

"Santiago, you're not taking anyone anywhere," Natalie ordered firmly.

"Natalie!" Camila shouted, angry at her inconsiderate attitude.

"They're boyfriends, don't you see?" Natalie screamed at her mother-in-law through tears.

Camila, shocked, grabbed Lincoln by the arm, and as she looked at him, the truth she feared was confirmed in his eyes. Immediately , she let him go in disgust.

When Santiago turned, he saw his mother release Lincoln with a look of repulsion and confusion.

"Lincoln, what did you tell her?" Santiago asked firmly, but Lincoln was preparing to leave.

"Mother, it's not true. What did he tell you?" Santiago asked, worried about being exposed.

"He told her the truth... that you're a faggot," Natalie screamed through her tears, savoring every word.

Santiago's vision blurred. Rage, shame, and confusion swirled inside him, and without thinking, his hand crashed against Natalie's face. The echo of the slap rang out in the room, cutting through the tension like a sharp blade. Natalie stumbled, bringing her hand to her cheek as she fell to the floor.

"Santiago, no! She's pregnant!" Camila cried out, running to help her daughter-in-law.

Stunned, Santiago stepped back, trapped between what he had done and the fear consuming him. The truth hit him like a punch, making him retreat even further, as he began to cry like a child upon seeing his girlfriend lying on the floor. Unable to bear it and consumed by a thirst for revenge, he let the anger take over as he stormed out of the house. Outside, the snow fell in thick flakes, and Lincoln, with sharp pain around his chest that made it hard to breathe, walked away from that house in Astoria and all the drama he hadn't caused but would always be remembered for. Each step reflected the unbearable pain, so he reached out for the ketamine in his pocket, and before inhaling the white powder to regain his power, Santiago appeared behind him and shoved him with such force that Lincoln fell on his stomach, and a scream escaped as if all his ribs had been ripped out. Santiago, without mercy, placed his foot on Lincoln's neck, pressing just enough to keep him pinned down, but not fully crushing him.

"What did you say to my mother?" Santiago growled, his voice thick with rage and anxiety, loaded with a dangerous intensity. Lincoln breathed with difficulty, unable to form words under the pressure of Santiago's foot. Desperate, Santiago pressed harder, but Lincoln seemed uninterested in defending himself, further fueling Santiago's rage. So he flipped him over roughly to face him, torn between the love he never dared to admit and the hatred that now consumed him.

"Tell me what you said to my mother!" Santiago shouted, his voice breaking, the sound desperate and wild. In the distance, Camila's scream: "Son, no!" announced her imminent arrival.

Under the pressure of his mother's approach, Santiago pressed down harder on the injured area, demanding an answer.

"What did you tell my mother?"

"I told her the truth," Lincoln gasped.

"Faggot!" Santiago spat on him as his mother grabbed him by the arms and pulled him away.

And when they were gone, Lincoln lay there in the snow, the cold seeping into his bones, extinguishing the fire of his broken ribs. For a moment, he closed his eyes, imagining the quiet indifference the snow could offer him, far from the chaos that haunted him. Lying on the ground, he looked around for where the *ketamine* bag had fallen, and when he found it, he noticed it was far away. He sighed, disappointed, as his desire to remain still competed with his urge to consume the drug. While debating between satisfying his need or his desire, he watched the snow fall romantically, slow and silent, and from all the things he could have thought at that moment, the one that came to him with a touch of nostalgia was: "What a beautiful night to die."

As the seconds passed, the ground that had once lulled him into a romantic calm now slowly dismembered him in a cycle of hypothermia. He dragged his body toward the bag of *ketamine* and inhaled deeply as if his life depended on it. Exhausted, Lincoln decided to order an Uber, resolved to continue the night and find comfort in an adventure he promised himself would be unforgettable.

Meanwhile, Santiago returned home with Camila. Francisco stood at the door, a leather belt dangling from his hand, stirring old memories for Santiago. The last time his father had punished him like *this*, Santiago had been barely thirteen years old. He had stolen a dollar from his mother's change after being sent to buy the missing ingredients for lunch. When Camila discovered the theft, she confessed it to Francisco, and the punishment was harsh: they made him kneel on metal *Coca-Cola* bottle caps until the skin on his knees bled. The lashes that followed left his back and legs marked for weeks. That was the last time Santiago dared to take something that didn't belong to him. But this time, the punishment wasn't for a childish act of disobedience. Natalie had stirred a suspicion that Francisco had buried for years. In a trembling voice, she confessed to having seen Santiago and Lincoln kissing outside the bathroom of one of the nightclubs they frequented. Francisco, his patience frayed and rage barely contained, confronted his son with a question. The answer ignited a fury he tried to release through whipping his son. But instead, he received a punch landing squarely on his face.

That Christmas Eve, Santiago left the house aimlessly, before his father could kick him out. Camila, filled with disappointment and shame, didn't stop him. Natalie, disgusted, ended their relationship.

The Uber driver was a lonely 40-year-old Guatemalan who had decided to work on Christmas Eve because he had neither a girlfriend nor a dog to celebrate with. When he arrived, he noticed that the person he was picking up wasn't doing well. He got out of the car and helped him up. Lincoln was hunched over, tightly holding his broken ribs, struggling to breathe. Once inside the vehicle, Lincoln longed for the days when breathing was as simple as breathing. And in the midst of the struggle, he had a conversation that the driver would never forget for the rest of his life. Lincoln told him how he had met Derrick and how, for no apparent reason, he had lost him. He also recounted how, coincidentally, he later met the woman who would become his wife and the mother of Derrick's child, who now would be his child.

"Where's Derrick?" the driver asked, intrigued and confused about whether he had followed the story.

Lincoln shrugged, wondering the same.

"And the mother?" the driver pressed, even more intrigued.

"They're both dead," Lincoln answered, deep sadness in his eyes.

The driver parked the luxury SUV and looked into the backseat, searching Lincoln's eyes.

That night, before heading out to work, he had looked at himself in the mirror with resentment, feeling old, lonely, and ugly. Resigned to his ugliness and inevitable unhappiness, he grabbed his car keys and headed into the city to make some money and feel less lonely. But when he looked into Lincoln's eyes, he couldn't help but feel a deep pity for him and an overwhelming gratitude for the life he had.

Before stepping out of the car, Lincoln pulled out his bag of *ketamine* and respectfully asked if the driver minded if he used it in his presence. The driver didn't object, nor did he respond with words, as he was still processing the story Lincoln had shared.

"Guatemalan," Lincoln began, "promise me you'll never do drugs," he said, inhaling the *ketamine* with the power of a brand-new vacuum. He had taken more than he should have, but not enough to leave him in a temporary vegetative state.

"Why don't you quit, friend?" the driver asked, concerned.

"Because I'm an idiot," Lincoln replied with a fake smile, the quick effect of the drug setting in, as he watched the long line of men, freezing in the cold, desperately waiting to get into the nightclub—where he used to work, back when this whole story began.

"You really should quit for good." The Guatemalan said, in all seriousness.

"I'm quitting tomorrow," Lincoln shot back, pulling out a small leather wallet from his coat pocket. The wallet, with its metal zipper, fit perfectly in his closed hand. He opened it, revealing party drugs neatly packed in small plastic bags, placed the bag of *ketamine* inside, and zipped it shut. Then, he hid it in his underwear, between his testicles. The Guatemalan looked at him confused of his action, but Lincoln smiled kindly at his innocence. He then took *two* $100 bills from his wallet and handed them to him, wishing him a Merry Christmas. Lincoln exited, a brief exchange of glances with the driver before heading straight for the VIP entrance, the line behind him disappearing as he slipped into the club's fervor. All that night, the Guatemalan couldn't stop thinking about the story of that handsome and generous young man. And, as time passed, every once in a while, he would remember him with nostalgia.

———

Outside the nightclub, the thermometer read a chilly 28 degrees Fahrenheit. With high expectations, New York City anticipated that temperatures would drop to -1 degree as the night went on. Meanwhile, inside the venue, under a suffocating and stifling atmosphere, more than 1,000 people attended the event with tickets purchased online; another 150 bought theirs at the box office, and approximately 50 managed to bypass security and enter for free. This caused the club to far exceed its maximum capacity.

Seduced by greed and taking advantage of the massive turnout, the club owners decided to turn off the air conditioning as a strategy to boost drink sales, breaking a record for the number of water bottles sold. However, many of the attendees, determined to reach the bar to hydrate or mix their drugs with liquids, found themselves trapped in the middle of the dance floor. Amidst the oppressive heat and deafening music, some opted to dehydrate or take their drugs without any liquid, while others chose to hydrate at the mercy of strangers or with the saliva of unknown people.

In the end, this wasn't just a party, but rather a congregation of attractive and athletic men, aged between 26 and 50, coming from different parts of the world, sharing a single objective: to hunt other men for sexual consumption, whether in private encounters or group dynamics.

After midnight, Lincoln entered the club where he used to work when this whole story started. By 1:30 a.m., he found himself alone, somewhat intoxicated, in the privacy of one of the bathrooms, consuming his set of drugs: ketamine, GBL, and euphorix, as if security personnel cared. Occasionally, though, they did care, dragging unconscious men through the crowd using wheelchairs and straps to transport those who had overdosed on recreational drugs. These people were taken to a restricted area, with stretchers lined up against the walls, where they were left to sleep off the sinister effects of the substances. Upon waking—anywhere from forty-five minutes to two hours later—they were released, almost sober, wrapped in a sense of shame, wondering how they had ended up there. But that confusion quickly faded as they rejoined the party, which invited them to keep consuming, whether for what was left of the night or the morning, or what was left of their lives.

At 2 a.m., Lincoln left the bathroom, energized. He bought a bottle of water and drank it all in one go, without pause. Then, without much expectation, he ventured into the crowd on the dance floor, standing out as the only one who chose not to remove his shirt, hiding the bruises on his body numbed by the drugs. Not recognizing anyone and feeling alone, he began to think, and in the midst of his thoughts, he pulled out his phone and started writing in his notes app: "I HAPPENED WHEN YOU SAW ME..." But after the first sentence, nothing else made sense; the mechanics of his fingers disconnected from his brain.

Visibly intoxicated and submerged in that sweltering sea of sweaty and drugged men, Lincoln, in a desperate attempt to breathe, stood on his toes, trying to snatch the dense air floating above their heads. It was at that precise moment, as he struggled to catch a breath, that his phone slipped from his hands and fell to the floor, unnoticed by him or anyone else.

As the minutes passed, the air inside the club only grew thicker, the heat more unbearable. Lincoln, now drenched in sweat, pushed his way through the pulsating crowd, barely able to stay on his feet. His mind was racing, not quite coherent, but still aware enough to feel the intensity of the moment. Every beat of the music thudded against his chest, every flash of light searing through his haze. He moved aimlessly, losing track of time, losing track of everything, the drugs and exhaustion dragging him deeper into a spiral of disorientation. The heat clung to his skin, and his head spun with a dull, persistent throb. For a moment, Lincoln wondered if this was it.

Suddenly, someone grabbed him by the shoulders, and Lincoln opened his eyes, startled.

A figure leaned in close, a man whose face he couldn't recognize because it appeared deformed before him. He said something, but Lincoln couldn't make it out over the music. The man's hands lingered on Lincoln's shoulders as Lincoln failed to recognize him. He tried to move, to shake the stranger off, but his body felt heavy, like he was stuck in slow motion. The man leaned in again, whispering something incomprehensible in his ear.

Panic rose in Lincoln's chest, and in the confusion, the man slapped his face. Staggering backward, Lincoln tried to make sense of what was happening, but then, through the haze, he recognized Santiago's worried face.

"Santiago?" Lincoln muttered, his voice barely audible over the thumping music. Without warning, he hugged Santiago, clinging to him as if his safety depended on it. His grip was desperate, hands trembling as he held on tight, seeking something solid that could prevent him from collapsing.

Santiago stiffened for a moment but didn't push him away. Instead, he sighed in evident frustration. "What did you tell her?" Santiago asked, his voice tense, still upset. Lincoln hugged him even tighter, the weight of his guilt pressing down on him.

"I'm sorry," he whispered, his voice full of remorse.

"Lincoln?" Derrick's voice cut through the tense embrace, breaking the moment. Lincoln froze, his grip on Santiago loosening as he slowly turned his head toward the sound. His eyes, wide and disoriented, met Derrick's worried gaze. The confusion on Lincoln's face deepened, unsure if what he was seeing was real. His vision blurred, and everything felt distant, like a departing rocket at full throttle, like a dream he couldn't wake from and a smile he couldn't wipe off.

Derrick, immediately noticing the signs of Lincoln's overdose, gently pulled Santiago aside. His face hardened with concern as he leaned closer to Lincoln, checking his pupils with the expertise of someone who had done this before.

"Are you okay?" Derrick asked, his voice calm but full of concern as he took in the sight of Lincoln, overdressed in the oppressive heat of the club, his skin clammy and his breaths shallow.

"I'm better now," Lincoln thought he said, but no words escaped his lips. He simply stared at Derrick, a silly smile plastered across his face as he struggled to breathe in the thick, stifling air. But the moment Derrick lifted Lincoln's arms to remove the t-shirt over his head, Lincoln screamed at the top of his lungs, a raw, desperate sound that pierced through the noise of the club. The panic in his voice was undeniable, causing those nearby to glance over.

Derrick knew something was wrong. Instinctively, he ripped off the t-shirt to reveal a massive purple bruise around Lincoln's rib, alongside several newer bruises scattered across his torso. The sight made Derrick's stomach drop, and when he looked up at Lincoln, he noticed him struggling to catch a breath, desperately stretching above the heads of the crowd. But this time, it was different—he was suffocating.

With rising panic, Derrick grabbed a green inhaler from his fanny pack, bringing it urgently to Lincoln's mouth. Lincoln inhaled deeply from the inhaler, feeling the flashes of light crashing against his face, illuminating the night. In that instant, he heard, soft like a whisper, the melody of *'The Beauty of Falling,'* as if it were being played just for him. As the air filled his lungs, his eyes found Derrick's face once again, almost forgotten among the memories he never let die. He smiled, and as he exhaled so deeply, his body surrendered, collapsing as the world around him faded into absolute darkness.

That night, during the fourteen-hour event, thirty-five men were taken unconscious to the emergency room, where most were treated and allowed to re-enter the party. Five of them were escorted out, but only one of the thirty-five was taken by ambulance due to a low heart rate, oxygen deficiency, and lack of vital signs, which forced the paramedics to intubate him dramatically in front of shocked onlookers after a traumatic CPR session. Amidst the commotion caused by the arrival of the ambulance, Dj Vortex stopped his playlist for thirty-five seconds, causing confusion in the crowd, but he was quickly compelled by the event organizers to continue before chaos ensued.

Of the more than a thousand people who attended, few witnessed the unfortunate sequence of events that led to Lincoln's imminent collapse. Although rumors spread in various parts of the party that someone had died on the dance floor, this caused curiosity but no surprise, as the vast majority of attendees were aware of the dangers of their party choices, and Santiago was no stranger to this reality. After leaving his parents' home and seeking temporary refuge at one of his former classmates' houses, now without family and without his best friend, Lincoln, Santiago decided to attend *"The Last Party at The Saint"* alone and consume euphorix to escape la mala noche. However, no matter how much he consumed and despite the turmoil in his head, the drugs had no effect.

On his way to the bathroom, Santiago was drawn in by an unusual commotion. As he approached, curiosity mingled with dread, and he caught sight of Lincoln—whom he hadn't seen since that fateful moment just hours earlier at his parents' house—lying on the ground. A team of paramedics surrounded him, their faces set in intense concentration, while three club guards formed a protective barrier around the scene.

"Lincoln!" Santiago shouted, his voice cutting through the chaos, heart pounding in his chest as fear gripped him. He took a step forward, urgency propelling him, but one of the guards immediately extended a strong arm, halting his progress.

"He's my friend!" Santiago implored, desperation lacing his words as he struggled against the overwhelming anxiety clawing at his insides.

"Your friend?" the guard echoed skeptically, his stance unwavering.

"Yes!" Santiago replied, panic rising in his throat. His eyes widened in horror as he watched the paramedics perform chest compressions, each push a race against time. He prayed silently with every compression, hoping to feel the spark of life return to Lincoln's still form. As the moments stretched into infinity, Santiago felt as though the world around him had fallen away, leaving only the sound of the frantic heartbeat of his fears.

When Lincoln finally gasped for air, a ragged breath that signaled his return, Santiago exhaled a sigh of relief so deep it felt like a renewal of hope. Yet, as he stood there, rooted to the spot, unable to tear his gaze away from Lincoln's battered body, the sight of the bruises and the cold, lifeless motionlessness overwhelmed him. The paramedics prepared for intubation, the gravity of the situation weighing heavily in the air. Santiago's heart raced with a tumultuous mix of relief and dread.

SOMEWHERE, IN THE SNOW

*Nothing ever really goes away until it has taught
us what we need to know."* Pema Chödrön

At 5 a.m., Lincoln was admitted to Mount
Sinai West Hospital in critical condition, under
his birth name: *Pastor Sorni.* The doctors
connected him to a ventilator to stabilize his
breathing. Over the next few hours, they carefully
assessed the extent of his injuries and the effects
of the overdose. By 10 a.m., a specialized medical
committee met to assess his condition, which
had continued to deteriorate as the hours passed.
His numerous injuries and inability to breathe
independently forced the medical committee
to make a drastic decision: induce a coma. The
goal was to relieve the stress on his body, allow
his organs time to recover, and closely monitor

his condition while managing his breathing and pain.

Santiago, who had left his winter coat at the nightclub due to the urgency of the events, now in a sleeveless shirt and with his usual aversion to hospitals, leaned against the wall, holding Lincoln's belongings as he observed the silent suffering of the visitors in their eternal wait. As the doctors prepared to place him in a medically induced coma, the echoes of the night faded, leaving Lincoln in the quiet, suspended world between life and death. As he stood there, confused thoughts raced through his mind—how had Lincoln managed to hide his real name all this time? Just as Santiago pondered this, Kenny crossed his mind, sparking a sudden rush of anxiety. He quickly headed to the loft. Among Lincoln's belongings, he found the keys to the apartment. Upon opening the door, the silence invited him in, and the sunlight, streaming through the windows with the curtains wide open, enveloped him despite the 16 degrees Fahrenheit. It was a cold morning under a clear sky. The apartment wasn't completely organized, but it was clear that Lincoln had taken care to keep it clean.

Kenny was sleeping deeply in his crib, the windows covered. It was a sleep so unusual for him that it immediately alarmed Santiago. He knew Kenny's sleep had always been light and easily disturbed since birth. But something wasn't right this time. When he tried to wake him, Kenny didn't respond. With his heart racing, Santiago checked the boy's vital signs. They were slow, but how slow was too slow? How could he compare the erratic pounding of his own chest to the unnervingly calm rhythm of Kenny's? Unsure if it was normal, and suspecting that Lincoln might have drugged him, he quickly changed his clothes, wrapped the boy in a thick blanket, and rushed out to find a taxi, heading back to the hospital where Lincoln had been admitted.

The doctors found nothing unusual in Kenny's deep sleep. While his vital signs were lower than normal, they attributed it to his resting state and didn't consider it alarming. However, Kenny's evident malnutrition couldn't be ignored, which triggered an investigation that began to reveal a life marked by neglect and excess.

When Kenny finally woke up, Santiago was summoned by two doctors and a social worker. After a thorough review of Lincoln's case and his critical condition, the doctors decided to keep Kenny under observation for a few more days. Santiago tried to take temporary custody of Kenny, but his request was denied when it was discovered that he didn't have the financial means to care for the boy. However, he explained that he had access to an emergency fund from Lincoln, arguing that his late wife had left him enough of an inheritance to live comfortably for life. The doctors doubted at first, but Santiago's sophisticated appearance, wearing a *Balenciaga* collection jacket, made them reconsider. Despite their doubts, Santiago proved his close relationship with Kenny by showing over a hundred photos stored on his phone. Based on this evidence, the social worker agreed to grant him temporary custody, provided they made a visit to his home to assess the conditions. Santiago smiled, confident that there was no better place for Kenny than his own home and in his arms. In that, he was right, but what he never imagined was the unexpected surprise awaiting him with the arrival of the new year.

———

On December 31st, it wasn't even 9 a.m. yet when RedSaint, full of enthusiasm, was belting out *"Missing You"* by John Waite at the top of his lungs while driving upstate New York. Despite the cold morning, there was no sign of snow. When he arrived, he parked his jeep in front of a gray brick building that resembled the entrance to a clinic. And there he was, walking out of the building at just the right moment, as if it had all been perfectly timed. Seeing him, RedSaint flashed a smile filled with excitement. The gleam in his eyes made it clear how long it had been since they'd last seen each other. Derrick, carrying a rolling suitcase and a folder in hand, raised his arms in victory when he spotted RedSaint. Without hesitation, RedSaint jumped out of the car, and they both moved quickly, almost in a rush, meeting halfway. They embraced tightly, only pulling away when the warmth between them became impossible to ignore.

"How was prison?" RedSaint asked, his usual sarcastic tone cutting through the moment.

"Much better than Rehab," Derrick replied, dry but direct.

"Did you get raped?" RedSaint asked bluntly.

"They don't rape you in Rehab," Derrick answered as they both got into the car.

"But did you have sex in Rehab?" RedSaint pressed on, maintaining his provocative tone.

"No, no sex in Rehab," Derrick replied.

"That's why I'd rather go to prison," RedSaint quipped, smirking. Feeling a bit anxious, grabbed his vape from between the seats and tried to take a hit, but nothing came out. Annoyed, he asked Derrick:

"Hand me the pouch from the glove compartment."

Derrick opened the glove compartment and took out the pouch. Inside was the same green inhaler that Lincoln had used before collapsing at the nightclub. Derrick pulled out the vape and handed it to RedSaint.

"Take a hit," RedSaint offered, finally exhaling a thick cloud of vapor.

"No, I'm good," Derrick said, visibly uncomfortable.

RedSaint noticed the disconnect, and feeling slightly offended, sighed but decided to let it go. He knew Derrick always carried that gloomy attitude after getting out of Rehab.

"They don't let you smoke weed?" RedSaint asked, flashing a teasing smile, trying to ease the tension. He admired the sacrifice his friend made every time he checked into rehab, but he never understood why drugs affected Derrick so deeply. Unlike Derrick, he lived with the emotional coldness of a robot; when he felt down—something he rarely admitted—he simply medicated himself and went on with his day, pretending to be happy. But his greatest fear was that one day Derrick would realize the harsh truth about rehab centers—they don't work. And when that day came, he might consequently, unable to bear it, even take his own life

The silence in the car became unbearable, until Derrick suddenly broke it with an unexpected confession:

"I'm leaving New York," he said, as if he had made that decision long ago.

There was a newfound positivity and humility about Derrick, a departure from the pretentious air of a playboy, selfish prick. During rehab, Derrick underwent therapy almost daily, guided by an excellent therapist who excelled in the art of listening. Derrick opened up about his childhood trauma, and though not entirely cured, he learned an important lesson—one that would shape his perspective forever: "People don't go out of their way to hurt others; they go out of their way in the pursuit of saving themselves." This realization not only helped him understand his mother's and grandmother's choices, but also allowed him to connect with the struggles of his own choices on a deeper level.

RedSaint thought twice about moving out of New York City, then he agreed, with the condition of not moving to Texas or Florida or anywhere too hot in summer, as RedSaint couldn't tolerate the heat.

"You'll stay here." Derrick suggested.

"You won't survive without me." RedSaint retorted.

"This time, I think I will." Derrick confidently replied, locking his eyes with him, with such confidence that it agitated RedSaint.

In a fleeting moment, RedSaint lost control of the Jeep, abruptly stopping it. Derrick, anticipating what was coming, felt an urgent need to breathe, so he jumped out of the car; RedSaint, fueled by rage, followed suit.

"Are you going to leave me here?" RedSaint asked, a mix of incredulity and restrained anger in his voice.

Derrick didn't respond but vividly remembered the last time RedSaint *"abandoned"* him. It was the night of the incident with Kia, when RedSaint came home stumbling, under the effects of *euphorix* and other substances. He found Derrick curled up in a corner of the bedroom, his hands covering his face, while Kia's lifeless body lay on the bed. The scene was an impossible puzzle to piece together.

RedSaint's reaction was immediate. Without a word, he began packing Derrick's belongings with trembling but determined hands, throwing them into the hallway as if exorcising a ghost.

"Get out," he said, his voice a mix of rage and desperation.

Derrick, paralyzed, barely understood what was happening. It wasn't until hours later, from the shadow of a tree across the street, that he fully grasped it. He watched as RedSaint, standing at the door, welcomed the paramedics, playing the role of a heartbroken lover while they carried Kia's body away. That night, RedSaint took full responsibility, leaving Derrick with an emotional debt that RedSaint never collected, but that Derrick carried like an invisible weight—one that not even all the money or gold in the world could repay.

Back in the present, Derrick looked at RedSaint but couldn't find the words to explain that the time had come to separate their lives.

"I can't stay in New York," he finally said, ashamed, avoiding his gaze.

Derrick had considered many reasons to leave, but he had only found one to stay—one that would ultimately destroy him.

"Then we'll go together," RedSaint replied, searching for approval in his eyes.

Derrick remained silent, struggling with the lump in his throat. RedSaint had been both the best friend and the worst accomplice. From the day they met, when Derrick was 14 and RedSaint 18, he had been a constant presence, shaping Derrick's life in ways he could never have imagined. He was the one who brought him to the set of *"Under The Brooklyn Bridge,"* convincing the producers that Kenny, an unknown teenager, could replace the deceased star. He was the one who paid for his plane ticket from New York to Los Angeles, freeing him from the oppression of his grandmother. He was the one who introduced him to luxury and opulence, teaching him how to navigate a world as seductive as it was dangerous. But RedSaint was also the one who dragged him to the bottom. The same friend who saved him also ruined him. The drugs, the nightlife, the reckless decisions... Everything good and bad about Derrick was owed to RedSaint. And for that, despite everything, Derrick could never forgive him.

"You and I... no, I can't anymore," Derrick finally said, with a firmness that felt like a stab in the back to RedSaint.

RedSaint's face hardened. He stepped toward Derrick, his gaze full of reproach, and for a moment, Derrick thought he was going to hit him. But RedSaint stopped, his anger transforming into something else.

"You're a thief! And a murderer!"

Derrick looked at him, incredulous, as if he had been slapped.

"It was an accident," he said defensively.

"No, an accident is when you crash your car or forget your keys at home. What you did, Derrick, wasn't an accident. It was cowardice."

RedSaint stepped back, his voice trembling with fury.

"Do you know what an accident is? It's when your best friend, almost like a brother, the one who's shared his whole damn life with you, has to clean up your mess, carry a corpse, and lie to a judge to save your ass. So you could pocket 1.5 million dollars. And what did I get in return?"

Derrick turned his gaze away.

"I never asked you to do those things for me," he muttered, ashamed.

RedSaint let out a dry laugh.

"You didn't need to, you idiot," he spat, his voice breaking at the end. "But now I see that to you, it meant nothing."

He turned toward the car but stopped halfway, as if there was still something left to say. He turned his head toward Derrick, his expression a mix of fury and pain.

"You're a liar. You always thought you were better than me, but I built everything for you. I gave you a home. I gave you a future. You're nothing without me, Derrick Passeri. Nothing! And wherever you walk, you'll always walk in my shadow."

Derrick remained silent, because anything RedSaint said was true.

"Now go and die alone, you ungrateful bastard," RedSaint spat, before turning back to the car and slamming the door shut.

The engine roared as RedSaint drove off, but a few meters away, he stopped abruptly next to Derrick. He rolled down the window and looked at him with a mixture of contempt and bitterness, as if he had one more blow he couldn't hold back.

"Remember Lincoln, the toilet cleaner?" he said, his voice dripping with venom. "He's dying. Add that to your portfolio, asshole."

Derrick froze, the blood draining from his face. The impact of those words hit him like a bullet. Unable to fully process it, he ran toward the Jeep, searching for an explanation, a clue that would prove what he had just heard was false.

"Red! Wait! What do you mean?" he shouted, his voice breaking with desperation.

But RedSaint didn't respond. He rolled the window up quickly and sped off. Derrick ran a few steps after the vehicle, his mind struggling to understand, to cling to something that could undo the weight of that revelation. But the Jeep disappeared into the distance, taking with it any hope of answers. Derrick stood by the roadside, the cold wind biting at his skin. And yet, he felt a strange sense of release. It was an unfamiliar sensation, a stillness that promised something greater. Maybe peace, he thought, though he didn't yet know how to hold on to it. But the moment faded as quickly as it came, interrupted by the echo of RedSaint's words: *"He's dying."* Urgency wrapped around him like a heavy blanket. This time, he couldn't look the other way. From the back seat of the Uber that finally picked him up, Derrick began to piece together the puzzle. RedSaint wasn't someone who paid attention to insignificant details, much less to people who weren't part of his meticulously crafted world. If he knew something so serious about Lincoln, it could only be because he had witnessed it—a public disaster, impossible to ignore, even for RedSaint. He thought of the only places they could've crossed paths: *Dean's Dungeon*—where Lincoln had last found him in a sex swing—or maybe a massive party. Both events often took place in Hell's Kitchen, and if something serious had happened, they'd have taken Lincoln to the nearest hospital: *Mount Sinai West*. He called the hospital, but the receptionist told him twice that there was no patient registered under the name Lincoln. Frustrated but convinced the woman hadn't checked properly, Derrick replayed RedSaint's words in his mind: *"Add it to your portfolio, motherfucker."* It was obvious he was implying that if Lincoln died, it would make two—counting Kia as well—both lost to overdose. So he decided to go directly to the hospital.

When he arrived, he asked again for Lincoln, but the receptionist insisted there was no patient with that name. Just then, Santiago emerged from the emergency room and overheard Derrick's frustrated conversation with the receptionist.

"Are you looking for Lincoln?" Santiago asked, approaching Derrick.

Derrick looked at him and, noticing his accent and Latin features, nodded.

"Lincoln Sorni?" Santiago asked, making sure they were speaking of the same person.

"You know him?" Derrick asked, not really knowing Lincoln's last name but clinging to a hope, as if he'd found something lost long ago.

"I do know him," Santiago replied, studying Derrick carefully. "But who are you?"

"I'm Derrick," he said, extending his hand toward Santiago.

Santiago couldn't—and didn't try to—hide his surprise and confusion. Not after having read Lincoln's writings and convincing himself that he was the "Derrick" who inspired each word. Now, standing before a Derrick who was possibly the real one, he felt the weight of betrayal and disillusion crushing him.

"How do you know Lincoln?" Santiago asked, his tone cold and calculating, masking the wave of emotions surging within him.

"An old friend," Derrick replied, nonchalantly.

"What happened to him?"

"Are you *his* lover?" Santiago asked bluntly.

"Is that what he told you?" Derrick replied, uncomfortable, trying to keep his composure.

Santiago studied him, sensing the shades of an emotion neither of them could put into words.

"What happened to him?" Derrick insisted.

———

Derrick's gaze remained fixed on the X-ray of Lincoln's broken ribs as Dr. Shiowanna meticulously explained the factors that had exacerbated the rapid decline in his health. The untreated broken rib and the lack of oxygen at the scene had worked against his recovery. Derrick drifted into thought, imagining all the ways he could have prevented the series of unfortunate events if he had been there. He also recalled that other winter night, as cold as this one, when he found Lincoln abandoned at the rusty bus stop, unconscious and at the mercy of the night.

"Is he going to die?" he asked abruptly, cutting off the doctor's report.

Dr. Shiowanna paused for a moment, taken aback by the direct question.

"We're doing everything we can," she finally replied.

"That wasn't my question," Derrick said sharply.

The doctor looked at him intently, realizing that he was the kind of person who valued simple questions and short answers.

"Do you believe in God, Mr. Passeri?" Dr. Shiowanna asked.

———

When Derrick was seven years old, back when he was still called Kenny, his mother left him at his grandfather's house. Until then, he had never had the privilege of meeting his grandfather in person, but he knew all about him from his mother's bitter stories. She never ceased describing him as a despicable and tyrannical man. However, that day, out of necessity, she took him there, promising to return for him before nightfall. The grandfather, uninterested in entertaining him, carried on with what he would have done regardless: reading. Kenny, bored of being bored, approached the old armchair and interrupted his reading. The old man offered him the book to read, but Kenny asked for money in exchange. The grandfather accepted the bribe, but when he realized the boy couldn't read, he found, in that moment, not only a connection with the blond-haired child but also a purpose.

The next morning, only little Kenny awoke. Alone and bewildered, he prayed to God to bring his grandfather back, but his prayers were answered in reverse, as he soon discovered that his mother wouldn't return for him either. From that day on, Kenny decided never again to bother God with his affairs.

———

After checking his watch, Santiago felt compelled to interrupt, recalling a commitment that couldn't wait.

"Damn, I need to go pick up Kenny.

"Kenny?" Derrick turned to him, clearly unsettled by hearing his former name.

Dr. Shiowanna stepped in, cautioning,

"Santiago, with the baby, I can't guarantee your visit to Pastor tonight."

"Pastor?" Derrick, annoyed, turned toward her. "Stop calling him Pastor, his name is Lincoln."

"Actually, his full name is Pastor Sorni," Santiago confirmed calmly.

"And who is Kenny?" Derrick asked, now even more confused.

"Pastor's son." Santiago said, sarcastically.

"What?" Derrick was left speechless.

The night fell before 5 p.m. Kenny was wide awake and animated in the arms of the social worker, who had been looking after him as if he were her own. For New Year's Eve, and as had been arranged, Santiago would assume custody of Kenny until Lincoln awoke from the coma or until his case was resolved. Kenny clung tightly to Santiago, but his eyes remained fixed on Derrick. The child observed him with an intensity that went beyond mere curiosity, as if searching for something familiar in the man's face. Derrick, feeling Kenny's persistent gaze with those blue eyes like his, began to grow uneasy. He tried to look away, but each time he glanced back, he found the child watching him with that same inquisitive expression, as though Kenny were attempting to recognize something lost in the folds of his memory. Santiago, attentive, silently observed the strange connection that seemed to be forming. Derrick felt a discomfort he couldn't quite explain—a tingling in his stomach that left him unsettled. The child stirred something entirely new within him, a mix of nostalgia and unease. Finally, Kenny offered a small smile, and in that moment, Derrick felt as if something inside him trembled, touching something very deep.

"Any plans for the night?" Santiago asked as they walked toward the hospital exit.

"No," Derrick replied, realizing that for the first time in years, he had no plans for New Year's Eve.

"Where do you live?" Santiago asked.

"Not far from here."

"We're in SoHo. You're welcome to join us if you'd like."

"SoHo?" Derrick raised an eyebrow, surprised.

"Actually, it's Lincoln's place."

"Lincoln lives in SoHo?" Derrick repeated, surprised by the exclusivity of the area. "That kid! His name is not Lincoln, he has a son named Kenny, and he lives in SoHo."

"He's also a widower," Santiago added to Derrick's report. "His wife drowned the same night they got married."

Derrick took a moment to absorb the wave of information he'd just received.

"Pastor..." he murmured, feeling a strange sensation as he said the name. After a moment of silence, Derrick asked, "Did Pastor have issues with drugs?"

Santiago sighed, the truth evident in his expression.

"Did you say his last name is...?"

"Sorni," Santiago responded.

"Pastor Sorni..." Derrick repeated, trying to recall where he had heard that name before. He pulled out his cell phone and stepped away from Santiago to make a call.

"Hi, Ryan, I won't take up much of your time. Could you confirm if the name of the patient who was supposed to be under my guidance, but never showed up, is Pastor Sorni?"

As part of the rehab program, those who had reached a certain level of sobriety were encouraged to mentor new patients. Ryan, who had been closely involved in Derrick's recovery, had suggested that even though Derrick hadn't quite met the required timeframe, this experience could help solidify his own progress.

"Give me a moment..." Ryan replied, checking the records. "Yes, that's correct."

"Could you send me his photo?"

"What's going on?" Ryan asked, puzzled.

"Just send it, please. It's urgent."

Derrick hung up the call, eyes fixed intently on his phone screen, waiting for the typing indicator to appear in their chat. Finally, the dots appeared, and soon after, a photo of Lincoln, taken from Pastor Sorni's file, filled the screen. Derrick enlarged the image, feeling a knot form in his stomach, and sank into a silence heavy with disbelief.

Sometimes, the greatest turning points in life aren't the ones you see coming—they're the quiet, invisible moments, when the smallest choices slip by. In those fragile spaces, lives are reshaped, and everything you might have been is left somewhere, waiting, in the shadows of *what could have been.*

"Are you coming?" Santiago asked.

"I'd rather stay the night." Derrick replied.

———

Derrick and Dr. Shiowanna walked down the hallway, but he slowed his pace as they approached the room, feeling an unease he couldn't shake off. Upon entering, the doctor noticed that Derrick hadn't followed; when she turned back, she found him standing still, caught in a mix of fear that contrasted with the raw firmness he had projected since she'd met him. Realizing his own exposed fragility, Derrick composed himself and entered.

Unexpectedly, the room wrapped him in a warm atmosphere that seemed to emanate life. The soft light softened the space, casting deep shadows. As Derrick moved closer, his eyes traveled over Lincoln's body, lying covered with a blanket, until they settled on his face at rest. He observed the fine, clear texture of his skin, contrasting with his dark hair scattered messily over the pillow. His long lashes cast delicate shadows on his cheeks, shielding those eyes that, although now closed, had once cried for him upon seeing him stripped of all dignity, abandoned to the mercy of others on that sex swing. The curve of his full lips, which, when not smiling or moving, seemed to silently beg for one of his kisses. The shape of his cheekbones and the serenity of his sleeping expression gave him a peace that, had Derrick felt it sooner, he might never have left.

Derrick sighed, enveloped in a melancholy that awakened as he realized that, holding Lincoln's hand, he felt a firm squeeze.

"He squeezed me!" Derrick said, a spark of emotion in his eyes.

"He knows you're here. Just talk to him," Dr. Shiowanna encouraged, her smile gentle.

Derrick hesitated, his voice caught between the danger of speaking and the safety of silence. Words felt almost too intimate, as if they might unveil something he wasn't prepared to face—or perhaps he simply didn't know what to say. Finally, he decided to reside in the quietness. Dr. Shiowanna observed him with curiosity and compassion, trying to decipher the nature of their relationship.

"He's a very handsome man," Dr. Shiowanna said, breaking the silence and joining Derrick's contemplation.

"From the very *first day*," he replied without hesitation, his gaze lingering as he continued to study Lincoln's face.

Dr. Shiowanna didn't look away from him. There was something in the way he gazed at Lincoln that unsettled her.

"He's also very smart. Did you know he is writer?" She asked him.

"He mentioned once that he wanted to write a novel" Derrick said

Before he finished, Dr. Shiowanna placed a manuscript of around 80 pages on the bed, next to him.

Derrick, intrigued, read the page that covered the manuscipt: *The Man I Adored*, accompanied by notes from the nurses and doctors who had taken the time to read it. Messages like: "You are gifted, Little," "What a beautiful story, such a writer," and "Reading your work is better than watching a film" filled the margins. Others wrote, "Please come back—I want to read more of you," and "You've touched something deep. Thank you. —Dr. Shiowanna."

"In every way, he wasn't a simple man, and how could he be?" she recited.

Derrick looked at her, bewildered.

There was no doubt that Lincoln had become the favorite patient in the intensive care unit. On numerous occasions, Santiago had pleaded with Dr. Shiowanna to take special care of him— not only because of his young age or the infant son waiting for him, but because Lincoln was a promising writer who deserved a chance to be discovered.

Dr. Shiowanna, at 46, had gone through two divorces that ended in courtrooms. She had two sons, but one of them had rejected her—a rejection she had herself provoked by failing to accept his sexual orientation. Her only faithful friend, an old golden retriever who had been by her side for over two decades, had eventually required constant care. She had reduced her hours at the hospital to devote more time to him, but the loneliness and inevitable erosion of her sense of purpose led her to make a heartbreaking decision: to put her beloved pet to rest.

Santiago, recognizing Lincoln's talent, printed a copy of *The Man I Adored*, and in a deliberate oversight, slipped the manuscript into her bag with a note that said: In hospitals, people die every day. Writers like Lincoln, not so often.

When Dr. Shiowanna found the manuscript tucked into her handbag, her eyes lingered on the name: *Lincoln (Pastor Sorni)*. She hesitated to read further, but the title: *The Man I Adored,* unsettled her—it hit too close to home. She had adored men her entire life, but they had all proved her wrong. Still, the first few lines hooked her instantly: *"In every way, he wasn't a simple man, and how could he be?"*

Dr. Shiowanna didn't hate her son, but in quiet moments, she found herself questioning God, wondering why she'd been given a gay son instead of a straight, football-playing heartbreaker. She harbored a twisted envy toward mothers with rebellious sons and difficult daughters-in-law. Her own sons caused her little trouble—except for the gay one, who, on a rainy day, had looked her dead in the eye and said, "You either accept me for who I am, or you can go and f** yourself." She had taught her sons to be impeccable with their words. Clearly, they'd learned well—especially him.

Still, she couldn't put Lincoln's manuscript down. The prose was so vivid, so raw, that the world outside those pages faded into an almost forgotten memory. When she finished reading, her mind a swirl of emotions, she instinctively called her son. He didn't pick up, and thank God he didn't, she thought.

The Man I Adored had struck her on a level she wasn't prepared for. By the time Derrick stood silently in front of Lincoln's sedated body, nearly everyone in her unit had read the manuscript too. And like her, they couldn't shake it.

Derrick looked confused after Dr. Shiowanna recited, "In every way, he wasn't a simple man, and how could he be?" In his eyes, she saw a glimmer of unfamiliarity—he had no idea about *The Man I Adored,* let alone that he might be the inspiration behind those pages. Her intuition whispered that he likely had no clue Lincoln was a writer. Just as she considered explaining, a nurse interrupted, requesting her assistance elsewhere.

"Can I stay the night?" Derrick asked as she turned to leave. Alone with Lincoln, Derrick had the chance to truly see him, to reach out, to speak to him. But he didn't. Those gestures weren't in his nature. Instead, he did just one thing: he stayed. Present. With all of himself, he hesitated before reading the manuscript. Finally, he turned the page, revealing the second one, and began to read:

In every way, he wasn't a simple man, and how could he be?...

How should I start telling you my sad story?

Maybe, I should begin with the day when I was misplaced, and then thrown out from my mother's womb. Or perhaps, rather, I should begin with the day when I saw him for the very first time.

Life was trash before him, and
uncertainty right after...

A faint memory surfaced—Lincoln's voice, a
quiet promise made one late night. *"One day, I'll
write something for you, and you will read it."*
The words on the page brought that moment back
with startling clarity, a whisper from Lincoln
that seemed to reach across time, bridging the
silence between them. For the first time in so
long, Derrick felt Lincoln's presence so vividly,
as if the words on the paper were breaths taken
for him alone. And with that, almost convinced
to dig into the manuscript, Derrick sat down.

Outside, New York City shimmered, bustling
as it always does every New Year's Eve. Just
blocks away, thousands gathered to witness the
ball drop in *Times Square*. Yet from Lincoln's
window, the view felt both private and quiet,
almost sacred.

Before he ever opened Lincoln's manuscript,
Derrick had only read one book in his entire life:
"Anna Karenina." He truly hated it, yet it lingered
like a ghost—haunted by the unforgettable
shadow of Anna herself.

When I saw him for the very first
time, I was behind the bar slicing
lemons after picking up the trash.
Despite the cold winter outside,
I was sweating inside like a pig.

I should have been salty, like
sweat, but I swear I smelled like
something else—like cum: the smell
of puberty.

He didn't smell like puberty,
though, because he was a man, and
men don't smell like cum.
Men smell like men.

I cut my finger that night
looking at that man, and I would
gladly have cut my hand; if I could
have an infamous piece of him.

Derrick smiled, captivated by the storytelling.
He remembered that day as if it were yesterday,
but was surprised Lincoln hadn't mentioned
seeing him on the train, thinking he was the first
to notice him.

Wether big or small as a peanut,
a kind boy should have heroes.

I never had heroes myself,
because those meant to protect me
couldn't even protect themselves.

When I first met my hero, in the
snow, I was still kind, though no
longer a boy.

~~Six men~~, if I recall, took me by
surprise and dragged me into the
darkest night.

I wish I could remember what
they did to me, and why they did it,
but an abducted memory is like a
street with no entry.

Or maybe, I forgot to remember.

If none of this had happened
that night, I might never have been
saved by my ~~private~~ hero."

Derrick couldn't reconcile with the
memories the passage brought back. He closed
the manuscript as quickly as he could, unwilling
to read any further. Since the day the incident
took place, he'd tried countless times to forgive
himself for what he'd done. He'd tried, too, to
ask Lincoln for forgiveness, but the words never
came easily, leaving him only with thoughts that,
even to this day, kept him captive. And as much
as he wished he could shut it all out, he found
himself drawn back, unable to resist the need to
know it all.

If you haven't been betrayed,
then you haven't lived enough. And
If you haven't truly been in love,
then you haven't been hurt enough.

That day, I was high in the clouds; he was down underground, stretched out like a sacred deer.

I remember how I got there, but I can't recall what I expected to find.

Six men had him—maybe they were more, but I like to think there were six. It was too dark to count, and I was too high to try hard.

Despite the darkness, he looked at me with those ~~evil~~ blue eyes.

Part of me wished he were in danger so I could save him, but men like The Man I Adored are a danger only to themselves.

He never said he loved me— not because he didn't feel it, but because the tight conduct that drove his emotions towards the face of his tongue was absurdly amputated.

He loved me silently, because once he tried to love me loudly, he destroyed me.

Derrick felt exposed. Reluctantly, he let his mind drift back to that day at *The Dean's*

Dungeon. Witnessing Lincoln's breakdown there had shattered any appeal the place once held for him. Now, the thought of those visits made him sick. If he'd ever loved that place, it was only because, down there in the shadows, men could portray their ugliness. These men secluded themselves in the darkness of a basement, rather than under the brightness of the flashing lights.

He looked out the window at the crowds gathering to welcome the New Year—the most exciting night in the world. But here he was, sitting alone, waiting for some kind of absolution. He turned back to Lincoln, lying motionless, as if time hadn't dared touch him. Quietly, Derrick read the line again to himself: "He loved me silently, because once he tried to love me loudly, he destroyed me."

Derrick had never known how to love, and at this point, he wasn't sure who to blame for that.

If my mother knew that I married a woman, I'm sure she would have published it in the town newspaper. And when no one cared anymore, she would have framed it and hung it in the living room next to my father's picture... And if my mother knew that I married a woman with more money than the mayor, I'm sure she would want to be my mother now. But I no longer want to be her son.

When I discovered that K was
his son—not my mother's, but his—
his son was already mine.

Although my wife never longed
for a baby, I dreamed of one that
looked like him.

Blessed must be the bitter flesh,
for, unwittingly, I ended up being
the father of his child.

Oh, poor wife of mine! Who loved
me with such blind devotion.
I prefer to think that, more than
loving me, she loved all my broken
parts, and in her attempt to piece
them back together, she ended up
breaking herself.

Oh, my God! How cruel death is
when it abandons us in the shadows
and leaves us at the mercy of so
many broken questions.

Derrick read the passage one more time,
finding the revelation jarring, his breath catching
as he tried to wrap his head around the words
on the page. Kenny was his son? It didn't make
sense. He hadn't been with a woman—he would
have remembered, at least that much. His grip
tightened on the manuscript. Was Lincoln lying?
Or maybe Lincoln believed it himself. Derrick

had no idea. But deep down, something gnawed at him—doubt.

For the first time since he'd started reading, he questioned not just Lincoln's version of events, but reality itself. How could this be true? His mind spiraled as he looked again at the description of Kenny—the golden hair, the blue eyes—remembering Kenny's stare toward him when they saw each other for the first time. Could a child who resembled him so perfectly really be his? Or was this another cruel twist in Lincoln's chaotic narrative?

What if Lincoln had simply believed it because he needed to? Because he needed something to tie him and Derrick together. These thoughts narrowed his perspective, pulling him deeper into the story. He had no choice—he had to keep reading.

```
      You might think that hitting
rock bottom happens once, and boom!
You're broken into pieces. But that's
not how it is!
      Every morning, I wake up with
the night... and I think: Maybe today
will be the day I find my way out,
or my way in... Maybe today will be
the day everything changes, and in
the end, nothing changes.
      Just more of the same.
      I used to know what I wanted.

      I neglected my wounds to trade
them for new ones.
```

I spent entire days lost in ketamine, which over time has rented me anxiety and an addiction that now costs me more than I can afford.

With black ink, I fill entire pages.
I talk to him in solitude during my nights and days, which are also my nights.

Waiting for a response, I remain in expectation, if not for his voice, then at least for some whisper from the wind. But in this house, not even the wind has shown itself in a long time.

I've seen on the NEWS that in the city people die from an overdose every day. Why them and not me?

One of these days, they'll break down the door to my house and find me lifeless in some corner where I used to consume ketamine, while I spoke to him and wrote the memories of my life.

If an overdose doesn't exterminate me, surely it will be loneliness or the damn ketamine that accompanies me daily without fail.

And what can I say about my poor son?

I feel sorry for him, born to a father who didn't even know he existed and a mother who, in life, didn't want him...

I feel so much pity for my poor son, who at such a young age already had to settle for me to save him from his moribund life.

Oh, poor God, who knows so little about life. To place a life in my hands when I can barely figure out what to do with my own.

Derrick's hands trembled as he reached the final words. Lincoln's closing thoughts left him breathless. This was more than just a story; it was a life unraveling before his eyes, and he had been both a spectator and a participant.

Lincoln had poured every last ounce of himself onto the page, laying bare his soul in a way Derrick had never imagined. The realization that he hadn't just hurt Lincoln but had been part of the wreckage that followed him overwhelmed him. He was struck by the thought that his existence, something he had never fully considered, had damaged someone so pure and innocent. And yet, as much as the manuscript played out Lincoln's pain, Derrick couldn't help but wonder: What was real? What had been blurred by Lincoln's longing? Where did the fiction end, and the reality begin?

The weight of uncertainty pressed down on Derrick, leaving him to question everything he thought he knew. Lincoln's words haunted him, and now Derrick realized that whatever happened next, he couldn't turn away—not from Lincoln, not from the boy, and not from the truth of their intertwined fates. Holding the manuscript, Derrick shifted his gaze to Lincoln, searching for answers. That's when he noticed Dr. Shiowanna standing beside him, like a silent apparition. Their eyes met, and in that brief moment, they both held the same unspoken questions: Who was Derrick in Lincoln's life? Who was truly Kenny's father? And, most disturbingly, what would happen next?

"This can't be true," Derrick muttered, his voice shaking with disbelief.

"So why do you look so affected?" Dr. Shiowanna asked, her eyes fixed on him, searching for something deeper.

Derrick, still in shock, slowly closed his mouth, unsure how to respond.

"Why did you leave?" Dr. Shiowanna pressed, a question she'd wanted to ask long before meeting him.

"I could've killed him if I stayed," Derrick admitted, the truth spilling out, even to himself.

"You should talk to Santiago," Dr. Shiowanna advised, her voice soft yet firm. "He would know more than anyone else."

Derrick didn't know if he wanted to know more.

———

At 10:30 p.m., Derrick stood at a crossroads, torn between seeking the truth from Santiago or answering RedSaint's relentless texts, urging him to join a massive New Year's Eve party. The kind of party that draws in all kinds of men—the ones who party every weekend, the ones who show up once in a while, and the newcomers who've never partied before. He hadn't replied, but the temptation gnawed at him. A part of him wanted to be there, sober as he claimed, just to feel the buzz of the crowd, to soak in the energy that could be invigorating. But deep down, all these were just fantasies of good faith. When he walked out of the hospital, RedSaint was waiting, cellphone in hand.

"Hey!" RedSaint called out, approaching from behind.

Derrick turned but didn't stop walking, surprised by RedSaint's persistence. It was clear from the start—RedSaint was desperate.

"What are you doing here?" Derrick asked, his annoyance clear.

"I'm looking for my friend," RedSaint shot back, ironically.

Derrick felt guilt gnawing at him. He knew RedSaint so well—over two decades of friendship—and yet, he had never seen him look so alone.

"I'm not going out," Derrick warned him.

"One cocktail to celebrate, nothing crazy... then we can go home and watch a movie."

Derrick couldn't help but smile sarcastically.

"You never go home before sunrise."

"You've never visited anyone at the hospital," RedSaint countered.

Derrick paused, turning to face him fully, guilt flickering in his eyes. After a brief moment, he finally said, "I'm sorry, man. I've got plans." Then, without waiting for a response, he turned away and kept walking.

RedSaint seethed—not because Derrick had plans, or even called him 'man' (which he never had before)—but because he said "I'm sorry." It was like Derrick didn't care anymore—as if RedSaint meant nothing to him now. As if Derrick had found something better.

"You motherfucker!" RedSaint snapped. "What's your plan, huh? Let me guess—feeding a vegetable?

"He's not a vegetable!" Derrick shot back, spinning around and spitting the words in his face, jabbing two fingers hard into RedSaint's chest.

"C'mon, Derrick! He's dead, and if they haven't unplugged him, it's because the faggot's got nobody."

"He's got his friends. He's got everyone in there caring for him.

"His friends? What friends? I brought him here! I found him all fucked up on the dance floor, I gave him my inhaler, and I *fucking* saved him. No friends showed up. And if everyone liked him there is because of the stupid diaries.

"It's called manuscript!" Derrick corrected him, feeling smart. "How do you now about the manuscript?" Derrick asked, intrigued.

"Everyone knows about it."

"Did you know that he had a son?"

"Which son? The one that he fucking drugged so he could go out and get high. He's been drugging his son since, probably, since he was born. He's a fucking *addict,* and he better never wake up."

Derrick punched him square in the face.

"And what are you, huh?" Derrick screamed, his voice trembling with anger.

RedSaint didn't expect the punch. Even though he could've hit back, he didn't.

"Who the fuck do you think you are?" Derrick shouted, eyes blazing with fury. "Just because you manage to function doesn't mean you're *not* a drug addict. In fact, you're the worst of us."

"The worst of us?" RedSaint muttered.

"Don't play the fool, Saint." Derrick let out a bitter laugh, more to himself than to his interlocutor.

"Recreational on weekends, functional during the week. Steroids for the muscles, Viagra for sex. You are the biggest lie I've ever known."

"And what about you, *Saint* Derrick? What about you?" RedSaint retorted, his voice loaded with venom.

Derrick looked at him, getting close enough for his words to feel like a knife between them.

"Me? I never pretended to be anything else."
For a moment, time seemed to stop. The remark hit harder than a punch. RedSaint, who had always prided himself on his ability to walk the tightrope without falling, felt how Derrick had just unmasked his survival strategy. But instead of responding, he looked away, as if the confrontation had reduced him to nothing.

"Maybe it should be you who never wakes up one day," Derrick concluded, and with that, shut him down and walked off, leaving RedSaint under the streetlights.

The silence that followed was icy. RedSaint stared at him, trying to confirm if he had really heard those words come out of Derrick's mouth. But he found no trace of doubt or regret on his face. Derrick, without a single gesture of apology, turned and started to walk away, leaving RedSaint alone under the artificial lights of the city. Each step he took was an effort to contain the rage still pulsing in his chest, mixed with a pang of guilt that sank him while simultaneously freeing him. He felt the sting in his knuckles, though he wasn't sure if it was from the punch or from the cold seeping into his skin.

"We're not that different," he thought. But that idea, although true, filled him with a bitter disgust. He couldn't allow himself to think that; not now, not ever. He shook his head and forced himself to discard it, burying it in the darkest corner of his mind.

For his part, RedSaint stood still, processing the physical and emotional blow. It wasn't the pain on his face that paralyzed him, but the echo of Derrick's words, which pierced through the armor he had built over the years. He had spent his life functioning in a chaos he had created as a survival mechanism, and now, those words threatened to tear it all down. For the first time in a long while, he didn't know what to do or how to feel. Although he wanted to shout at Derrick, calling him by his real name: 'Kenny,' he couldn't, because his love for him was greater than the hate he had reserved for himself.

Times Square was nearly impossible to navigate—most streets were closed, and the frenzied crowd was pure madness. Derrick eventually broke free from the crowd, heading west toward the river. After a long wait, he finally managed to hail a cab, which took almost an hour to creep its way to SoHo through the dense traffic. As he stepped out, a strange feeling washed over him—a vague memory surfaced but nothing concrete.

"Look who's here," Santiago called out, crossing the street with Kenny in a stroller.

Derrick glanced over at them.

"I thought you weren't coming," Santiago said.

"Traffic!" Derrick started.

"I know. Tonight, everyone's excused for being late," Santiago replied, wearing a fine black coat that unmistakably belonged to Lincoln.

But Derrick wasn't listening to Santiago; his gaze was locked on Kenny's inquisitive eyes in the stroller.

Santiago picked up Kenny.

"Wanna hold him?" he asked, but before Derrick could react, Santiago abruptly handed Kenny over. Derrick instinctively caught him—it was either that or let the baby fall. The resemblance was undeniable. Santiago smiled knowingly, and in that smile, Derrick could see how much Santiago truly understood. Derrick's discomfort was palpable. Kenny's curiosity was immaculate. Suddenly, Santiago's phone rang. Without a word, he stepped away to answer it, his voice fading into the background. As the New Year arrived, the street erupted in cheers, people celebrating with joy. Derrick looked down at baby Kenny in his arms, and as always, Kenny's eyes were locked on his. Still unsure if Kenny was truly his biological son, Derrick couldn't ignore the pounding in his chest, an inexplicable pull he felt every time the child was near.

"Happy New Year!" Santiago said to Kenny as he arrived, having just finished greeting his family in Colombia—cousins and uncles—through a video call. He wrapped his arms around Kenny and hugged him warmly. Then, he turned to Derrick, and the two shared an awkward 'Happy New Year' embrace, the kind that made it uncomfortable to watch. Then he and Derrick headed up to the loft. For Derrick, everything felt like it was coming full circle. Just before entering, the name of the woman who had brought him there one intoxicated night resurfaced in his mind—"JoLynn," he muttered, recalling that morning when she mercilessly kicked him out because she wanted to sleep alone. Disoriented and out of his right mind, Derrick had wandered the SoHo streets aimlessly, unsure of where to go and looking like a homeless. It was only when his senses finally cleared that he realized he had no wallet or phone, but he still managed to hail a cab home. He was so embarrassed by the memory that he never shared the story with anyone.

"You know her?" Santiago asked, after hearing him thinking out loud.

Santiago, who had read the manuscript twice, still didn't know that Derrick had done the same. Curiosity gnawed at him—was it possible Derrick was really Kenny's father? He decided to gauge Derrick's reaction when he saw Jo Lynn's pictures. But there was no need for that. The moment Derrick stepped inside, the truth was already written all over his face. He stood at the door, stiff as a stone.

"You can leave if you want," Santiago offered, "and I'll never tell him you came back."

Derrick hesitated, the weight of the decision pressing down on him. It wasn't that he didn't want to be a father—he had wanted that for as long as he could remember. In fact, when he was too young to even know how babies were made, he would ask his mother at night, after everyone was asleep and she was washing the dishes:

"Mom, when am I turning fifteen?" he would ask, eyes wide with innocence.

"Not today, my son," she'd reply, her voice weary.

"But when?" he'd press again.

"I don't know, Kenny," she'd say, rolling her eyes.

"How come you don't know when?"

"Kenny, how many times have I told you to stop asking the same question?" she'd snap, frustrated.

Kenny would lower his head like a scolded puppy and start to walk away, but this time, his mother, hands still soapy, would grab his skinny arm and pull him back.

"Why do you wanna know when you'll turn fifteen?"

"So I can have a child," he'd say, tears brimming in his eyes.

His mother sighed, caught off guard by the answer.

"You don't want a child," she'd say gently.

"I *do* want a child!" he'd insist, his voice trembling.

"Why do you want a child?" she asked, genuinely curious now.

"So I can hug them and kiss them," he whispered, his tears finally spilling over.

That moment broke her. Despite her own struggles with substance abuse, she deeply loved her child. Her eyes filled with tears, and there, crouched down, she hugged him tightly and kissed him, whispering how much he meant to her. In that moment, her love was pure and true. But by the time Kenny became Derrick, those tender kitchen memories had faded into the blur. And now his biggest fear was harming his own son by his unsolved traumas. He didn't

245

feel ready to raise another human, and for what? To make him just to be like him? If his mother were alive, she would've tell him that nobody is ready to be a parent. That raising a child is like overcoming a drug abuse problem: you take it one day at a time.

Derrick, standing in front of Santiago and his son, faced an impossible dilemma: stay and try to be a father, or leave and live, only to die like a dog. No matter what choice he made, he knew he would be judged—either for leaving or for the inevitable mistakes he would make if he stayed. Believing in the promise that Santiago of no telling anyone that he was back, he turned away, and started walking away, along the hallway. Santiago swallowed dryly as he watched Derrick leave. In that moment, he couldn't fully understand why the disappointment gnawed at him so fiercely, especially for the immature actions of someone who was practically a stranger. But it all circled back to his friend Lincoln—who had tragically fallen for the wrong kind of man.

"Did you *rape* him?" Santiago's voice cut through the space between them like a blade.

Derrick stopped, turning back to face him. "I never touched him."

"That's right," Santiago snapped, his eyes blazing with anger. "Your friends did." His gaze locked onto Derrick's, determined to etch every detail of this moment into his memory forever.

When Santiago had first read Lincoln's manuscript, he couldn't bring himself to believe half of what was written. Knowing the emotional chaos Lincoln had endured, Santiago dismissed parts of it as fiction—an outlet for his suffering. But seeing Derrick's transformation upon stepping into the loft had shifted his perspective entirely. Derrick hadn't come just to visit; he had come to search for answers. And it was clear now that he'd found them.

Derrick stood there, ashamed, waiting for Santiago to say something more. But Santiago didn't speak. The silence stretched unbearably, and Derrick finally turned to leave.

"My girlfriend's pregnant," Santiago called out suddenly, his voice hard. "I'm going to be a father too," he said. "I'll take care of them with everything I've got, and I'll make sure none of them ever turns out like one of you." Without waiting for a response, Santiago turned and entered the loft, closing the door behind him with finality, leaving Derrick standing outside— alone, facing the sudden, inescapable void of his own existence. As he walked away, he wanted to cry, but the poor thing, didn't know how.

From the window, Santiago noticed that Derrick stayed on the street long enough, expecting, surely, not much. It was a cold night out, and Santiago's heart melted in the heat of the memory of that night when his mother screamed at the top of her lungs that he would be a father, as he punched his girlfriend on her face.

Santiago grabbed the keys, and with Kenny in arms, went downstairs to offer Derrick a place to sleep, suspecting that he might not even need it. Arriving to the firm soil, the night was still cold, but Derrick was gone.

———

There are *no* many things to do on New Year's dawn in Manhattan other than to join the ones already celebrating, or going to sleep, and Derrick was not ready for bed, so he decided to go out to party. The party was lit. Thousands of men welcomed the New Year with genuine excitement, riding the relentless waves of drugs. Derrick stood still in sobriety, scanning the crowd for RedSaint.

"Derrick?" *they* called out, strutting over in barely-there clothes—tiny on top, boots on the bottom, and something cropped in between. "What are you doing here? Welcome back. You look gorgeous," *they* said, without pausing for breath.

Though it was one person, *their* presence was bold enough to fill the room. *Their* gender wasn't up for discussion, nor was *their* sexual orientation—though *they* were clearly drawn to well-hung men.

Derrick forced a smile that looked genuine.

"Have you seen RedSaint?" he asked.

"He was just here," *they* replied, glancing around, clearly high. "If we stay put, he'll show up—I'm a hundred percent sure," *they* added, shifting *their* attention back to Derrick. "You look bored. What are you on?" *they* asked.

"Nothing," Derrick replied, his eyes still searching.

"That's why you haven't found him, honey!" *they* said, as *they* fumbled through their fanny pack. "What do you want? Ketamine, coke, ecstasy, molly, G, viagra or *euphorix*? I wouldnt do *euphorix* tho, that shit is insane and not in a good way; if you know what I mean. What do you need?"

"I'm fine, thanks," Derrick responded in a lower voice, as the craving inside surged stronger.

"You're *not* fine, darling" *they* said, still rummaging through *their* small fanny pack that was practically a mini drugstore. "Would you mind lighting up your phone?" *They* asked, trying to manage the dim lighting and *their* own drug stash. But Derrick didn't answer. When *they* looked up again, he was gone—disappeared completely off *their* radar.

———

On January 2nd, Derrick found himself lying in bed, his mind consumed by thoughts of his son and the cascade of unfortunate events. The TV was on, CNN flickering silently in the background. Derrick wasn't listening, nor watching. The world outside was noise—until it wasn't.

"Breaking News," the anchor announced. RedSaint's photo flashed on the screen. Derrick barely registered it when his phone rang, snapping him back to the moment.

He glanced at the caller ID and picked up.

"Derrick, is RedSaint with you?" RedSaint's mother's voice crackled with anxiety, trembling on the edge of panic.

"Yes," Derrick lied, instinctively. He always figured things out later.

"Thank God!" Her relief surged, but it was fleeting. In the background, another voice—frantic, worried—asked,

"Is he home?"

"Is he home?" she repeated, more urgently now.

"Yes," Derrick said, his heart beating faster, but his voice remained steady.

"Let me talk to him," RedSaint's mother demanded.

Derrick's eyes drifted back to the TV. His pulse quickened. RedSaint's picture—one Derrick had taken in Paris, 2014—was there, displayed beneath the headline.

His stomach turned cold.

"Derrick, put him on the phone!" her voice pierced the tension.

Derrick's hand shook as he turned up the volume on the TV.

"...a man has jumped from the 19th floor of a high-rise in Hell's Kitchen..."

His breath caught in his throat, goosebumps crawling up his skin. The phone slipped slightly in his hand as he remained silent.

The mother's voice on the other end shattered into screams, her words dissolving into raw, guttural sobs as the truth bled through the silence.

On New Year's Eve, after being punched by Derrick on the street. RedSaint, disappointed but promising not to ruin his special night, went out alone. As always, he found himself in the company of the old and a new group of men—strangers who, by the end of the night, he would call friends. And as it's expected, one party takes you the next one, and to the next one, and to the next, and when the energy drops, the drugs enhance it, and when the drugs ran out, you reload.

Just past midnight on January 2nd, RedSaint was captured by the security camera of a high-rise in Hell's Kitchen. His arms were crossed tightly over his chest, trying to shield himself from the biting cold. He had lost both his jacket and t-shirt somewhere amidst the many parties he had attended. His face, drawn and weary, seemed lost as he stepped inside.

By 6:00 a.m., the house party was at its peak. The apartment was packed so tightly with partygoers that the host finally announced, "No more entry, no re-entry." The air pulsed with laughter, music, and the low hum of half-shouted conversations.

At 6:15, RedSaint, wearing nothing but black boots and a leather jockstrap, stepped out onto the balcony to take in the frozen air. He was holding his phone, but he was so intoxicated that he couldn't even compose a coherent message to Derrick. He didn't seem to feel the cold, which would pierce the pores of any other mortal. He gripped the railing, and suddenly, the snow began to fall. Although he had known it for a long time, he had never allowed himself to contemplate it the way he did that morning.

At 6:18, another guest at the party, wrapped in a synthetic fur coat, stepped out onto the balcony to smoke. After finishing his cigarette, he instinctively looked down to toss the butt. What he saw made vertigo run through his body. A gut-wrenching scream escaped his throat, echoing so loudly that not only those on the brink of overdose inside the apartment woke up, confused, trying to understand what had happened, but also the neighbors in the buildings whose windows faced the epicenter of the catastrophe. So sharp and heartbreaking was that scream that people walking on the street stopped to look at the figure of the queer on the balcony of the nineteenth floor, covered in a synthetic fur coat, screaming at the top of his lungs. RedSaint's body lay motionless on the roof of the building's lobby, his eyes open to the sky, as if pleading for mercy from the infinite. Slowly, the snow began to bury him under a white blanket, leaving winter the task of silencing what hell had not been able to claim in its time.

RedSaint wasn't a bad man, but he lived much of his life with a blurred sense of identity, one that secretly developed from Derrick's rejection when Derrick was Kenny and both were young and painfully beautiful. That rejection put him on a dangerous path, twisting his anger toward young men with little to no experience with the dangers of nightlife. In permissive party environments, RedSaint would drug them, then take them away and assault them sexually, all under the guise of mutual consent. He used his good looks to draw them in, never pursuing them aggressively. After their encounters in the secrecy of the night, most of them came back to him, but by then, he had lost interest.

Derrick refused to believe that RedSaint had jumped. He didn't have a suicidal mindset, and even if he had developed one at the last moment, RedSaint wouldn't have done it without leaving a note—not after all the times he'd left post-its for Derrick on the fridge or scattered around the kitchen. Derrick's theories were simple: it was either an accident, or someone pushed him. He was certain more than one attendee at those parties would have pushed him from a higher floor without a second thought.

After learning of RedSaint's fate, Derrick couldn't find rest, couldn't sleep, haunted by the memory of their last argument on the street. He remembered his desperation to rekindle their friendship—and his own cold-blooded response. Regret gnawed at him. It felt brutally unfair, knowing RedSaint had never given up on him as quickly as he had. In the grip of guilt that burrowed too deep for tears or release, he craved a sliver of peace that only drugs seemed able to offer. And he didn't have to go far; every drawer in the house was filled with drugs. In that place, the kitchen wasn't for cooking; it was for preparing lines, for indulging. Derrick found himself at the counter, preparing a bump of ketamine from one of the bags in the drawer. But before snorting it, he slapped his face as hard as he could. Then, seized by a surge of rage, he hurled everything into the toilet and flushed it, watching as remnants of his pain washed away, learning that his battle was not against the drugs, but the loneliness and the night. The act stung with a bitterness that felt more like punishment than relief, but, at least in that moment, it was the only peace he knew. At his apartment, life constantly reminded him he couldn't be alone without someone watching or judging. It tested him endlessly. Under the pressure, he made a decision.

Meanwhile, at Lincoln's loft, life was tightening for Santiago. Although Hartford let him stay there until they knew Lincoln's fate, Santiago struggled with staying home all day at someone else's expense, solely to take care of Kenny. Determined to earn his own way, he returned to *Times Square*, working as a cosplayer, and earned a decent income. He even dressed Kenny in a cute Spider-Man costume, which drew even more attention. After his shifts, Santiago would go to the gym, carrying Kenny around like his gym bag. The days were short but full, and while some nights stretched long, he tired Kenny out so much that the toddler slept soundly each night.

Santiago couldn't visit Lincoln as often as he wanted, since Kenny wasn't allowed in the hospital, and each evening he would have to take Kenny to SoHo, hire a nanny, then return uptown to *Times Square*. Each day he planned to visit him, but Dr. Shiowanna advised him to stay home with Kenny, saying Lincoln was well looked after. But, on January 6th, Dr. Shiowanna asked him to come in as soon as possible. Santiago suspected he might have to sign paperwork to disconnect Lincoln, but when he reached Lincoln's room, he found Derrick there, asleep in a chair, his head resting on the bed while holding Lincoln's hand.

"He's here all day, every day," Dr. Shiowanna said softly. "He bathes him, trims his nails, brushes his hair. One day I even saw him brushing his teeth and applying serum to his face. He's barely sleeping."

An invisible thread bound Santiago and Derrick. Both were fathers pushed into their roles, both cast out of their homes for different reasons, yet by the same neglected spirit. And despite the odds, they felt not only guilt for what happened to Lincoln but an immense loneliness in the world. Still, Santiago had something to hold onto that Derrick had given him, something that kept him in survival mode.

When Santiago touched his shoulder, Derrick was startled, waking from a shallow sleep.

"You can't keep staying here," Santiago murmured.

Derrick raised his head, discovering his haggard and tired face.

"Why?" Derrick asked, confused, looking at Santiago and then at Dr. Shiowanna.

Santiago, not knowing what to answer, looked to Dr. Shiowanna, asking for her intervention.

Dr. Shiowanna forced an awkward smile and left.

"They don't like you being here all the time," Santiago hesitated.

"They haven't said anything," Derrick replied.

"They're too embarrassed to tell you," Santiago said. "Go home and rest a bit. I'll stay tonight."

"No!" Derrick exclaimed, agitated. More than a response, it was a reaction. "I'll stay here tonight. You go home."

Santiago noticed something wasn't right. He recognized fear in Derrick's face that he couldn't place and preferred not to probe further.

"You can't stay here!" Santiago concluded.

Derrick, channeling his frustration, gave Lincoln a handshake, stood up, and left.

Santiago watched him leave without regret.

Derrick stayed outside his apartment for about an hour. He knew that if he entered, this time, he would find a way to use. His life was so restricted that his sobriety was the only thing keeping him captive, and he needed to feel free, even if just for an instant, to continue the fight against his addiction. On the other side of the city, Santiago, lying in bed, couldn't fall asleep—the unprotected version of Derrick wouldn't leave his mind—when, suddenly, someone knocked on the door. At the door, Derrick, although standing upright, had his shoulders slumped. He had never felt so vulnerable or so exposed to rejection. Words weren't necessary. Santiago saw himself in Derrick's eyes and the fear they conveyed. At the end of the day, he too had no home, and nothing in this world belonged to him. So, he opened the door wide. That night, in Lincoln's marital bed, Derrick rested his head against Kenny's small belly, and Kenny, asleep, wrapped his little arms around his head in a comforting embrace. Santiago lay on the other side of the bed, and the three of them fell into a sleep as deep as Lincoln's, maybe not as deep.

––––

In the days that followed, without needing to discuss it, Santiago and Derrick naturally fell into a rhythm. Santiago would wake up around 6 a.m., make breakfast while Derrick showered. They'd sit down to eat together, sharing small talk—updates on Lincoln, casual comments like "Do you like your eggs sunny-side up?" Then Santiago would head to work, leaving Derrick home with Kenny. When Santiago returned at night, Derrick would go to the gym, then spend the night at Lincoln's side, either reading *Anna Karenina* aloud— he suspected Lincoln would appreciate the complexity of Anna's character and the story's dark undertones— or singing or doing just nothing. Eventually, he'd fall asleep beside him, only to rejoin Santiago and Kenny for breakfast. This routine worked well for them. But on the night of January 16th, as Derrick arrived at the hospital bundled in a black coat and wool hat against the first flurries of an approaching blizzard, Dr. Shiowanna intercepted him, her face alight with barely contained excitement. Outside, snow had begun to blanket the city, and forecasts warned the storm could last up to 72 hours.

"Lincoln woke up," she announced, breaking the tension in the air. Derrick's heart pounded so intensely he felt he might have a heart attack. Noticing his concealed excitement, she continued gently, "But during his recovery, his brain suffered some anomalies. It may take time for things to fully settle—or, they might not."

"Can he write?" Derrick asked, his voice tight, as if that were his only concern.

Dr. Shiowanna shook her head, her expression somber. "I'm afraid not, at least not for now."

Derrick absorbed the news, a pang of sorrow cutting through him. He knew Lincoln would feel lost without the ability to write. "Will he remember me?" he asked, hesitating.

"He'll remember the good things," she replied, offering a warm smile that made Derrick feel both safe and genuinely happy, a rare happiness that transcended any comfort he had ever known.

"Would you marry him?" she asked, the question cutting through the warmth of the moment.

Derrick blinked, caught off guard.

"If you married, Lincoln could access better medical assistance, which would greatly aid his recovery," she explained, outlining the benefits it would bring to Lincoln's challenging situation.

"Yes!" Derrick responded, his answer resolute.

"Are you sure?" she asked, wanting to confirm his commitment.

"Yes!" he repeated firmly.

"There's no turning back," she warned. "If you decide to marry him, it will be your responsibility. Lincoln is undocumented. Do you understand?"

"As long as he carries my last name," Derrick replied, his tone unwavering.

Dr. Shiowanna smiled, recognizing, beyond the pages of Lincoln's manuscript, the man Lincoln had chosen to adore. "Would you like to see him?" she asked gently. Derrick hesitated, feeling an intense mix of fear and shame.

The walk toward Lincoln's room felt endless. Derrick counted each step, missing none. Lincoln sat on the bed, facing the massive window, his back turned to the door. Derrick could hardly believe that the man he had cared for—lying lifeless like a fallen tree—was now sitting up on his own. As he approached, he saw Lincoln gently swaying his head, humming a melody. His eyes were fixed on the snow outside, flakes drifting down and tossed by the wind. A distant look held his gaze, as if he were in the most peaceful place on earth, untouched by reality. Derrick sat beside him and quickly recognized the melody

Lincoln was humming, the same one he had sung to him when he used to be unconscious. He smiled, settling into the peace Lincoln seemed cocooned in.

"Lincoln?" he called softly.

Lincoln continued humming, his mind lost somewhere beyond reach. Derrick, feeling a connection, began humming along with him.

As soon as Lincoln heard him humming, he looked at his mouth still.

"Lincoln, it's me—Derrick. I came to see you."

No response. Derrick's heart sank with worry.

"Lincoln, do you see me?" Derrick's eyes filled with tears.

Lincoln looked at him, but he was truly interested in those blue eyes filled with tears, containing a whole ocean within. Slowly, Lincoln lifted his hand, and as soon as he touched the tears, they fell like a cascade. Lincoln followed the tears, his gaze intent, as if trying to understand the meaning of that deep ocean.

Gently, he lifted Lincoln's chin, guiding his gaze to meet his own. Lincoln's eyes flickered but held no recognition.

"It's me, Derrick—your Derrick. Do you remember me?" Derrick whispered, his voice strained.

Lincoln seemed lost beyond reach.

"Why isn't he recognizing me?" Derrick asked, his voice edged with panic.

"Give him time," Dr. Shiowanna advised.

"I'm here with you, Lincoln," Derrick murmured, placing his bare hand on Lincoln's chest, feeling his own heart pounding beneath it. But Lincoln continued humming his melody, drifting farther away.

Derrick held his face again, his hands trembling. "Lincoln, it's me—the man you adored. You wrote it for me, and I've read it *all*. Please... say something." Tears filled Derrick's eyes, blurring his vision. Still, Lincoln hummed, but then, as if in slow revelation, he raised a hand to Derrick's cheek, touching a tear with quiet curiosity, as though he had never seen someone cry. The simple act broke Derrick's composure.

"Hi," Derrick managed to say through tears, his voice cracking. Lincoln shifted his gaze to Derrick's mouth, reaching out to touch his lips, as if discovering them for the first time. Derrick's heart swelled with a faint, fragile hope. "Hi," he whispered again, and for a brief moment, Lincoln's eyes met his, holding a glimmer of recognition.

Derrick smiled, leaned forward, wrapping his arms around him in a tight, desperate hug. "I love you," he whispered. "I love you, I love you... Please, tell me you still love me. Tell me, please!" His tears flowed freely as he held Lincoln close, then moved from his ear to kiss him softly on the lips.

"Derrick, no!" Dr. Shiowanna's voice cut through the moment, gently pulling him back. She placed a hand on his shoulder. "Derrick... he's gone."

Derrick's embrace loosened as he felt Lincoln slip, weightless, in his arms. Lincoln's face had turned pale, his expression blank and lifeless, his skin still warm, slowly, started turning cold to the touch. A wave of dread washed over Derrick. Grief, denial, and desperation clung to him as he begged Dr. Shiowanna to reattach the tubes.

"Derrick, he's gone!" She said again, her voice steady yet laced with grief as she tried to guide Lincoln's body from his grasp. Derrick clung to him, sobbing, refusing to let go.

"Please... please, the tubes! Put the tubes back on! He needs to breathe!" He pleaded, his voice raw.

"Derrick," she whispered, her voice laced with a grief reserved for someone she had come to know deeply, through every word of Lincoln's manuscript, *The Man I Adored*.

Two security officers entered quietly, prepared to pull Derrick away.

"Wait!" she said, raising her hand to stop them. "Derrick, you need to release the body."

"He is not a body! His name is Lincoln Passeri! And he needs to breathe!" Derrick cried, burying himself in his own tears.

Seeing his despair, Dr. Shiowanna signaled the officers to step back. Derrick finally released his hold, sinking to the floor behind the bed. Trembling, he pressed his lips to Lincoln's, breathing his own life into him one last time. Tears streamed down his face as he clung to the desperate hope that somehow, Lincoln would return.

Outside, a silent crowd had gathered—doctors, nurses, staff who had read and loved Lincoln's manuscript, *The Man I Adored*. They stood solemnly, listening to Derrick's final moments with him, their faces mirroring his sorrow.

That night, on Friday, January 22, 2016, Lincoln Sorni passed away in Derrick's arms. And as he departed, snowfall began, marking the start of a record-breaking blizzard in New York City, as if the sky itself mourned his passing.

LINCOLN PASSERI

"If I could die tonight; I promise myself to start all over again tomorrow." Lincoln Passeri

When Lincoln Passeri woke up, the world surrounded him

Watch the last chapter on a screen...
This story was always meant to be a film. Before
it became a novel, *All Nights Die Young* was a
screenplay—crafted to be brought to life on the
big screen. Now, that vision is closer than ever.

How You Can Be Part of It:

-Follow the journey – Stay updated on casting,
production, and behind-the-scenes content.
-Spread the word – Share the book, discuss the
characters, and imagine the world on screen.
-Support the project – Be part of the movement
to bring *All Nights Die Young* to life as a film.

Visit OurWebsite *www.voyaeonentry.com* to learn
more and be the first to know about the film
adaptation.

The most exciting thing about the end...
is the new beginning.

Stay tuned!

**Exclusive look
into the screenplay behind
*All Nights Die Young.***

INT. DERRICK'S BEDROOM - LATER

Techno on the speakers. Neon lights illuminate the room.

LINCOLN sits on bed. Grabs a photo-framed of a woman and a eight-year-old boy holding a guitar.

                    LINCOLN
          Your mother?

DERRICK on his knees, focused, doses with a dropper two drinks with a suspicious amber bottle.

                    LINCOLN (CONT'D)
          Where's she?

                    DERRICK
          Connecticut.

                    LINCOLN
          You play the guitar?

                    DERRICK
          Not anymore.

                    LINCOLN
          Do you sing?

                    DERRICK
          What is this, a goddam interview?

This changes the good energy.

                    LINCOLN
          I write.

                    DERRICK
          You're a writer?

                    LINCOLN
          No! I only write.

                    DERRICK
          You write Mexican.

                    LINCOLN
          Spanish, you mean?
              (beat)
          No, I don't like to write in
          Spanish. I write in English.

                    DERRICK
          How can you write in English when
          you barely speak it?

                    LINCOLN
          Maybe One day you'll read my work
          on The New Yorker.

DERRICK sighs, making fun of him as he finishes pouring GBL in the drinks. He hands him one of the shot glasses.

                    DERRICK
          The New Yorker? He's delusional,
          and no, I'm not gonna read it
          because I hate reading, but good
          luck... I believe in you.

DERRICK cheers and drinks it all at once. LINCOLN mimics him.

                    LINCOLN
                  (excited)
          Do you?

                    DERRICK
          No, I don't fucking care.
                  (beat, bored)
          Get naked. I wanna see what those
          steroids did.

                    LINCOLN
                  (takes off his t-shirt)
          What's your dream?

                    DERRICK
                  (travels his fingertip
                  across his torso)
          My dream is to die young.

LINCOLN freezes, not expecting that answer.

DERRICK, with a devilish grin, slips ecstasy into both their
mouths, followed by a swig from the bottle shaker, sealing
their daring pact.

                    LINCOLN
                  (optimistic)
          We should find a dream for you, and
          we could work it out together...

DERRICK studies his face, showing a sarcastic smile.

                    DERRICK
                  (playing with him)
          What would that dream be?

                    LINCOLN
          It depends on what you're good at.

                    DERRICK
          How you do it?

LINCOLN seems confused.

                    DERRICK (CONT'D)
          How can you bore me so easily?

LINCOLN, embarrassed.|

                    DERRICK (CONT'D)
          You know what.
                  (beat)
          I do have a dream.

LINCOLN tosses him a questioning face.

                    DERRICK (CONT'D)
                  (brings a bong from under
                  the bed)
          I want you to try this with me.

LINCOLN seems curious by the artifact (bong). DERRICK grabs a
torch and lights up the bong's ball, smokes meth, offers it
to Lincoln.

                    LINCOLN
          I don't smoke.

                    DERRICK
                 (soft)
            That's why is my dream.

LINCOLN hesitates.

                    LINCOLN
            What's in it?

                    DERRICK
            Crystals.

                    LINCOLN
            Crystals?
                 (beat)
            Didn't know you can smoke crystals.

                    DERRICK
            You can smoke whatever you want,
                 (pointing at bong's ball)
            If you just put it in here.

LINCOLN smokes...

                    LINCOLN
            What should I feel?

                    DERRICK
            You should feel like if you've
            being cured from Gonorrhea.

                    LINCOLN
            Never had Gonorrhea.

                    DERRICK
            We gotta change that.

DERRICK throws himself at him, kissing him passionately.

Not all nights are meant to be survived

ALL NIGHTS DIE YOUNG

The journey begins now. **Follow the adaptation.**
www.voyaeonentry.com

More from
Mario Luxxor

THE
DAUGHTER'S
SUNSET
A SHORT-FILM

MARIO LUXXOR'S

LITTLE *DOG*
s short film with a *big* heart.

MARIO MEDINA, CHRISTIAN DELGADO, JAIRO BELTRAN, DANIEL GARCES, JENNY SEBALLOS, EDELINA VILLAMIZAR, RAQUEL GONZALEZ, JENNY LOPEZ, ARNALDO PINZON, FAMILIA MULIETH, LILIANA GOMEZ, SOFÍA GOMEZ, ANDRES PAJON, GLORIA HOYOS, BLANCA HOYOS, MARIERMA, JESÚS MULIETH, WILLINGTON REAL, GINA AVILA, MILENA GOMEZ, ALEJANDRO MOLANO, JACKELINE GALINDO, STEFANO AGUDELO

THANKS A LOT

Bebé

written and directed
MARIO LUXXOR

COURT MÉTRAGE
short film corner
FESTIVAL DE CANNES 2014

Made in the USA
Monee, IL
23 March 2025